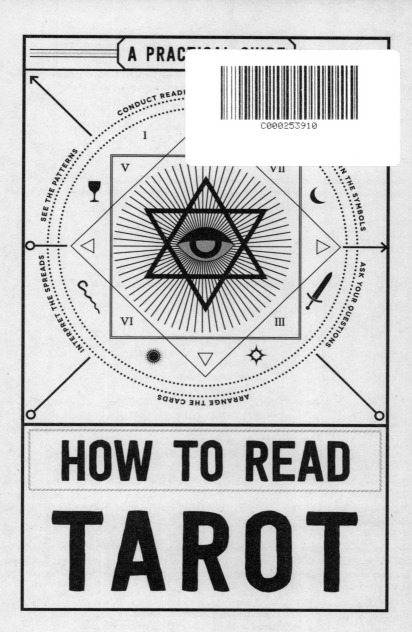

A PRACTICAL GUIDE

CONDUCT READING

SEE THE PATTERNS

INTERPRET THE SPREADS

ARRANGE THE CARDS

ASK YOUR QUESTIONS

IN THE SYMBOLS

# HOW TO READ

# TAROT

▲adamsmedia

AVON, MASSACHUSETTS

Published by
Adams Media, an Imprint of Simon & Schuster, Inc.
57 Littlefield Street, Avon, MA 02322.
www.adamsmedia.com

Contains material adapted from the following title published by Adams Media, an Imprint of
Simon & Schuster, Inc.: *The Everything® Tarot Book, 2nd Edition* by Skye Alexander, copyright ©
2006, ISBN 10: 1-59337-656-1, ISBN 13: 978-1-59337-656-7.

ISBN : 978-1-5072-0512-9
eISBN 10: 1-5072-0188-5
eISBN 13: 978-1-5072-0188-6

Printed and bound by CPI Group (UK) Ltd, Croydon, CR0 4YY

10  9  8  7  6  5  4  3  2  1

**Library of Congress Cataloging-in-Publication Data**

How to read tarot.
Avon, Massachusetts: Adams Media, 2017.
Includes index.
LCCN 2016042025 | ISBN 9781507201879 (pb) | ISBN 1507201877 (pb) | ISBN 9781507201886
(ebook) | ISBN 1507201885 (ebook)
LCSH: Tarot.
LCC BF1879.T2 H68 2017 | DDC 133.3/2424--dc23
LC record available at https://lccn.loc.gov/2016042025

Cover design by Stephanie Hannus.
Cover and interior images © 123RF/Daria Solomennikova.

*For information about special discounts for bulk purchases, please contact
Simon & Schuster Special Sales at 1-866-506-1949 or business@simonandschuster.com.*

# CONTENTS

### PART 1

## THE BASICS OF TAROT   9

### AN INTRODUCTION TO TAROT • 11

### INTERPRETING THE TAROT • 23

### SYMBOLISM IN THE TAROT DECK • 35

# THE MAJOR AND MINOR ARCANA  53

## MEANINGS OF THE MAJOR ARCANA • 55

## THE SUIT OF WANDS • 113

# THE SUIT OF PENTACLES • 129

# THE SUIT OF SWORDS • 145

# THE SUIT OF CUPS • 161

# PERFORMING TAROT READINGS 177

## HOW TO DO READINGS • 179

## TAROT SPREADS • 193

## SIXTEEN SPREADS • 207

## THE TAROT FOR PERSONAL DEVELOPMENT • 241

# INTRODUCTION

Reading Tarot cards is an ancient art. For centuries Tarot cards have been used as a way to interpret the self and predict the future. And you, too, can learn to read these mystical cards with just a bit of practice and some background knowledge. *How to Read Tarot* will show you how to interpret and understand the meaning behind Tarot cards. You'll find everything from explanations of each card in the deck to how to use the Tarot for personal and spiritual growth. Above all, you'll learn how to use the Tarot to discover your authentic self.

Your interpretation skills will grow with practice, so this guide provides you with information on over a dozen Tarot card "spreads"—groupings of cards—that you can use in a variety of ways to answer your questions. The more readings you do, the better you will become at sensing what the Tarot cards are trying to tell you.

As you become more familiar with the Tarot you'll find it easier to understand the cards and to detect patterns in them. The more you study and practice the Tarot, the deeper your understanding becomes and the more the cards will resonate to your inner life as well as to events in your outer life.

Now let's begin our journey through the wondrous and powerful wisdom of the Tarot.

### PART 1

# THE BASICS OF TAROT

# AN INTRODUCTION TO TAROT

For centuries, the Tarot has been used to see into the future and to gain advice on practical matters, such as a job, a marriage, or economic issues. Even today, these are perhaps its most common uses. But the Tarot can also serve as a tool to deepen your understanding of yourself, to enrich your relationships with other people, and to strengthen your connection with your Higher Self. Before you can begin your journey into reading Tarot cards it is important to know the history of the Tarot and also the practical matters of handling and caring for the special cards that you will use to stimulate your intuition and uncover the answers to the questions you have been pondering.

# HISTORY OF THE TAROT

Many theories abound about the Tarot's beginnings. One is that the great library of Alexandria in Egypt, whose female librarian Hypatia was world-renowned for her wisdom and learning, housed scrolls containing all the knowledge of the ancient world. Among these scrolls was the legendary Book of Thoth, derived from the mystery schools of ancient Egypt. The allegorical illustrations on Tarot cards are said to contain these secret teachings, which in the Major Arcana represent a course in personal and spiritual development. The Minor Arcana, which was added to the Tarot at a later date, may have derived from an Italian card game known as "tarrochi." Our present-day poker decks closely resemble the Minor Arcana of the Tarot.

The oldest surviving Tarot cards are from fifteen incomplete decks painted in the fifteenth century for the Visconti-Sforza family. These incomplete sets are referred to collectively as the Visconti-Sforza Tarot. No complete deck has survived, some sets have a few face cards, and some consist of only one card. The decks were all commissioned by the Duke of Milan, Filippo Visconti, and then later his son-in-law and successor Francesco Sforza.

Tarot images are inextricably linked to ancient beliefs, mythologies, and religious systems such as the Hebrew Kabbalah. The cards' numerological associations have been tied to the Greek mathematician Pythagoras, who taught that letters and numbers contain divine essence and extraordinary powers unrealized by the uninitiated.

Gypsies may have carried the cards to Europe. (The term "gypsy" is considered to be a corrupt form of the word "Egyptian.") The Catholic Church, however, believed the Tarot was "the devil's picture book," and the cards were quickly condemned as heretical. To possess them was dangerous. Thus, during the Middle Ages, the Tarot went underground, along with astrology and many other forms of occult knowledge. ("Occult" simply means "hidden.") Yet, despite persecution, the ancient knowledge contained in the Tarot continued to be passed down in secret, until interest in the cards surfaced again during the Renaissance.

Though we may never know their true history, we can still use Tarot cards to advise and guide us, to show us what lies ahead in the future, and to help us gain access to our inner knowing and the Divine. The amazing insights contained in the Tarot and the deck's inherent flexibility make it just as relevant to contemporary Westerners as it was to the ancients.

## EARLY TAROT DECKS

No one knows exactly where or when the Tarot deck originated. Evidence suggests that seventy-eight-card Tarot decks, much like the ones we're familiar with today, may have been used in Italy and France during the Renaissance for telling fortunes. During this period, the nobility in Milan used the Tarot for gaming and gambling.

It's believed that the first Tarot decks contained only the Major Arcana. Early packs portrayed people solely on the Major Arcana and Court cards. The numbered or pip cards showed only the suit's symbol—Cups, Swords, Wands, or Pentacles—in the corresponding quantity (One through Ten). Some decks didn't even include labels on the Major Arcana cards—perhaps because novices were discouraged from doing readings and adepts would recognize the symbolism without needing labels.

There are twenty-two cards in the Major Arcana. In the ancient study of numerology, twenty-two is considered a master number that resonates on the higher planes as well as the physical one. An extremely powerful number, twenty-two represents the master builder who can harness cosmic forces and use them to shape the world. The number of transformation, twenty-two also serves as a bridge between the earthly realm and the spiritual one.

## STORYTELLING DECKS

Storytelling images were added to the basic symbolism of the Minor Arcana cards in the first part of the twentieth century. Many of the most popular decks today, including the Waite deck and the Thoth Tarot, developed during this period. Instead of merely showing the appropriate number of symbols (Cups, Swords, Wands, or Pentacles) on the numbered cards, these decks portrayed activities or scenarios that described, through the language of pictures, the cards' meanings. People were depicted in relationship to the number of objects representing the suit.

These images made it easier to understand the meanings of the individual cards. For example, the vivid illustration on the Three of Swords—three swords stuck through a large red heart—certainly does convey a strong sense of heartache and suffering. However, some experts say the pip cards were illustrated as a memory aid rather than as an attempt to interpret the cards in a specific way.

One problem with specific illustrations, though, is that they may cause confusion. In some cases, an illustration may seem contradictory both to the meaning of the suit involved and to the number being represented. The graphic portrayals may also limit individual interpretation and free association. Not everyone interprets the cards in exactly the same way, of course, and the meanings can vary depending on the question asked. It's usually best to trust your own intuitive responses and to use the images on the cards as guides or prompts rather than as rigid definitions.

## THE RIDER-WAITE DECK

Since its introduction in 1909, the Rider-Waite deck (which is also sometimes called the Waite deck) has been one of the most influential and popular Tarot decks. The deck was illustrated by Pamela Colman Smith, a theatrical designer, artist, writer, and member of the occult Order of the Golden Dawn. The deck expresses Smith's knowledge of magick (spelled with a *k* to distinguish it from stage illusion and magic tricks) and mysticism. Guided by Arthur Edward Waite, she produced a series of seventy-eight allegorical paintings that included storytelling images on the Minor Arcana as well as the Major Arcana cards. Unfortunately, the innovative deck, which broke away from the standard Tarot designs that had been used for centuries, bears the names of Waite and sometimes that of its publisher, William Rider and Son, instead of Smith's.

More than six million Waite Tarot decks are now in print. Smith's original images have spawned numerous variations over the years, including the popular Universal Waite deck, brightly recolored by Mary Hanson-Roberts. Today you can buy miniature versions, over-sized versions, and even glow-in-the-dark versions of the Waite deck. This classic deck is widely used to illustrate books about the Tarot, including this one, and as a teaching tool for beginning diviners.

Some Tarot packs are designed especially for beginners. These decks provide keywords or written information along with images, symbols, and numbers to help novices learn the meanings of the individual cards. *The Beginner's Tarot* by Samantha Lynn, for example, is illustrated with simple line drawings that show the suit symbols, numbers, and a few words of explanation— such as "joy" and "pleasure." The Quick & Easy Tarot deck includes brief divinatory and reversed interpretations printed on each card, along with images from the Universal Waite deck.

## THE CROWLEY THOTH DECK

Another innovative and influential Tarot deck emerged during the early part of the twentieth century, birthed by a collaboration between the notorious British occultist Aleister Crowley and Lady Frieda Harris. Known as the Crowley Thoth deck, it features dramatic artwork, vivid colors, and striking imagery. The deck contains many Kabbalistic, magickal, and astrological symbols, as described in the Book of Thoth, which Crowley authored—hence the name of the deck.

Like the Waite deck, the Thoth deck has been reproduced in different variations and translated into numerous languages.

## VARIATIONS IN TERMINOLOGY AND NUMBERING

If you examine several different Tarot decks, you'll probably notice that they don't all use the same terminology. For instance, Wands may be called Rods or Staves in some decks. Cups are sometimes named Chalices, and Pentacles might appear as Coins or Discs.

---

In the view of alchemists and mystics, the symbols preserved and presented in the Tarot spring from the anima mundi, or soul of the world, a vast repository of knowledge, like a cosmic library, filled with all the memories and wisdom of the entire human race, past, present, and future. Sometimes called the Akashic Records, this source of knowledge could be accessed by anyone willing to make the effort to develop this psychic link to the source.

---

Figures in the Major Arcana often go by various names, too. The Hierophant, High Priest, Pope, and Jupiter are all names for trump five. In his Thoth Tarot, Crowley switched the names and the order of some Major Arcana cards. Instead of Strength, he gave us a card called Lust. The familiar Temperance card became Art in Crowley's deck, and Judgment was replaced with Aeon. The designers of some new decks take great liberties, renaming many of the cards and ordering them to suit their own purposes.

Some decks rearrange the numerical order of the cards. Strength and Justice (trumps eight and eleven), for example, are sometimes reversed. These unique approaches show the inherent flexibility that exists within the structure of the Tarot, which like any esoteric system of knowledge is enriched by diversity.

# CHOOSING A TAROT DECK

Whether you choose a standard deck, such as the Waite deck, a more modern deck, or one reproduced from a Renaissance pack, the decision is strictly up to you. So many wonderful and diverse decks exist these days, with new ones being introduced regularly, that the hardest part might be making up your mind!

## FINDING THE RIGHT DECK

Much will depend on whether or not you are primarily a visual person. The symbolism of the Major Arcana is pretty much the same in all decks, even if it is depicted through different themes (e.g., Celtic, Native American, Japanese, etc.). For some people, the pictures on the Minor Arcana serve as memory aids to the cards' meanings. Other readers prefer to dispense with storytelling scenarios on the Minor Arcana and are more comfortable with a simpler deck. In some decks it's difficult to tell immediately if a pip card is upright or reversed; in others it's obvious. Look at a number of decks and if one strikes your eye, try it out. Many stores keep sample packs available for you to examine and test before you buy.

When choosing a deck, bear in mind that in some decks the Minor Arcana cards are not to be taken at face value (when illustrated). There is no historical precedent for illustrating the pip cards; they are not derived from any ancient mystical tradition so far as historians can ascertain. Whether or not you choose a deck with storytelling images on these cards, interpret them first according to their suit and numerical divinatory meanings.

If after using a deck for a while you do not feel entirely comfortable with it and its symbols, get another deck. Feeling an affinity for the deck you are using is essential. You need a deck that will resonate with your own inner symbology, and that is compatible with your own belief system. Therefore, if the symbols make you anxious or uncertain, you have chosen the wrong deck. If you like the imagery—possibly crystals, animals, angels, herbs and flowers, or some abstract configuration—and if it seems to suit your personal point of view and you feel good using it, then you have found a good deck.

## USING MORE THAN ONE DECK

Many people like to have two or more decks, sometimes for different purposes. You might decide to keep one deck for your own spiritual development and use another deck for readings. These can be identical or of two different designs. If you read for other people, you'll probably want to have one deck for yourself and another for others to use.

If a deck in your possession does not seem right to you, lay it aside for a time. You can go back to it later on. During the interim, you may have changed, your intuition may have reached a different level, and the deck may work. If it still doesn't feel right, give it away or discard it.

Become thoroughly familiar with one deck first, using it until you understand the symbolism and can remember the meanings of the cards. Mastery of a single deck will make mastery of secondary or additional decks much simpler. The deck you begin with might not be the one you continue using forever. Many Tarot enthusiasts collect decks and may be proud of their libraries, but most have a favorite that they turn to whenever they want advice.

# HANDLING YOUR DECK

Handle your Tarot deck with utmost care and respect. Treat it as you would any precious possession of great value. Never leave it lying about unattended. Always return it to its special place immediately after you have finished using it for practice, meditation, or a reading.

It is important to clear the vibrations from your deck each time you use it, especially if another person handles the cards. However, if you use a totally separate deck only for your own spiritual practice it is not necessary to clear out your own vibrations. In fact, you want the deck to be impregnated with your personal energy. But, if you do readings with that same deck even if only for yourself, you should clear it after each reading so that no residue remains that might affect the next reading.

## BLESSING AND PURIFYING THE CARDS

It is a good idea to bless your deck each time before you use it. When you get a new deck, you may want to have a short blessing ceremony before you use it for the first time. This need not be complicated. If you already use blessing rituals as part of your usual activities, that will be sufficient. If you do not already have blessing rituals, simply place the cards in front of you, hold your hands palms down over them, and say, silently or out loud, "I call upon the divine powers to bless and protect these cards, for my intention is to use them for good only. I declare that only good shall come from their use and that all negativity shall be turned away from them."

There are many methods of clearing, or purification. The following methods are based on the four elements: Fire, Earth, Air, and Water.

✳ **Fire:** To clear with fire, you can place your deck of cards in bright sunlight for an hour or more. Or you can light a candle and set it in a candleholder on the table (or the floor—wherever you usually work with your cards). Lay your cards near the candle and allow it to burn beside them (being careful, of course, to watch over the process) while you silently invoke the Spirit of Fire, asking it to remove the old vibrations. Do not use the candle for any other purpose. If possible, put it in a glass receptacle that will enclose it entirely. When you finish clearing your cards, thank the Fire Spirit for its help.

✳ **Earth:** To clear with earth, use salt—preferably coarse sea salt (available in health food stores). For a salt-clearing, put your unwrapped deck into a small bowl and lay a sheet of clean white paper over it to avoid getting salt on the cards themselves. Make sure the cards are completely covered. Then, while silently invoking the Spirit of Earth, pour a layer of salt over the cards—on top of the paper—and leave it for at least twenty minutes. Afterward, pick up the paper with the salt on it and dissolve the salt in water. Pour the salt water down the sink drain (not the toilet) and run clear water after it. Give thanks to the Earth Spirit.

* **Air:** To clear with air, you can follow the Native American tradition of using smoke, called smudging. Smudging consists simply of lighting a bunch of herbs and wafting the smoke over or in what is to be cleared. Although different herbs are used for different purposes, sage is the most common. To smudge your deck, simply put a few sage leaves (or a heaping tablespoon of the ground herb) into a fireproof dish or vessel and set fire to it. When the smoke begins to form, hold the deck in the wafting smoke while you invoke the Spirit of Air. Do this for a few minutes until the smoke begins to dissipate. The beauty of the smudging technique is that not only do you clear your deck, you clear yourself and your room as well. Thank the Spirit of Air.

* **Water:** Clearly you cannot soak your deck of cards in water, but you can create a water atmosphere with a mister. Simply fill the mister with pure water (distilled or from a spring), invoke the Spirit of Water, ask it to cleanse and renew your cards, and then spray-mist the air above and around you. Misting produces negative ions that literally change the energy in a room. When misting, use the finest spray you can, sending light puffs of mist into the air above your cards. Be careful not to get them wet. Give thanks to the Spirit of Water.

## SHUFFLING THE DECK

Most Tarot decks are larger than a deck of ordinary playing cards. A new deck will be stiff and usually slick because the cards are treated with a protective lacquer-type coating. You will need to break in a new deck just as you must break in a new pair of shoes. Ruffle the cards at the edges a few times to give them flexibility. In time, as you handle the cards, they will become softer and easier to use.

◇◇◇◇◇◇◇◇◇◇◇◇◇◇◇◇◇◇◇◇◇◇◇◇◇◇◇◇◇◇◇◇◇◇◇◇◇◇◇◇◇◇◇◇◇◇◇◇◇◇◇◇◇◇◇◇◇◇◇◇◇

When doing readings for other people, you can let them decide how they will handle the cards. Some people are shy, reluctant, or unsure. You can tell these people to simply hold the entire deck in both hands while they formulate clearly in their minds what they want the reading to achieve for them. Then you do the shuffling.

◇◇◇◇◇◇◇◇◇◇◇◇◇◇◇◇◇◇◇◇◇◇◇◇◇◇◇◇◇◇◇◇◇◇◇◇◇◇◇◇◇◇◇◇◇◇◇◇◇◇◇◇◇◇◇◇◇◇◇◇◇

How you shuffle the cards is up to you. Shuffling, cutting, and handling the cards puts your individual vibrations onto them, so they can absorb your energy and respond to your concerns. Perhaps you've seen psychics read a person's life from a piece of jewelry or other personal object; the principle is similar. Most Tarot readers have a special method or ritual that allows them to connect with the cards, whether they are reading for themselves or for others. In time, you'll probably develop your own. Whether you cut, tap, or blow on the cards, the object is to establish a link between yourself and the oracle.

Oversized decks are difficult to shuffle overhand, as you might an ordinary playing deck (the way a professional card dealer shuffles). You may prefer to hold the pack in one hand and with the other slide out small sections and reposition them, doing this several times until you feel the cards are well mixed. Some people spread the cards out and stir them around with both hands. A third possibility is to cut the cards into several stacks, restack them, cut into more stacks, restack, and so on until you feel right about the amount of mixing you have done.

Whether you allow anyone else to shuffle or touch your deck is a matter for you to decide. Some card readers ask the person for whom the reading is being done to handle the cards (whether they simply hold them, shuffle them, cut them, or mix them in another manner) to put their personal vibrations on the cards. But other readers adamantly refuse to allow anyone else to shuffle (or handle) their decks. If you decide to allow others to handle your deck, use one of the methods given previously for purifying the deck in between users.

Before you handle your deck, be sure to wash your hands thoroughly in warm water, preferably with a sweet-smelling, pure soap. Soap made from glycerine or vegetable oils is the best because it contains no animal products. Dry your hands on a soft towel and lightly apply some neutral greaseless lotion to them. Treat your hands with care and respect, for they are the physical conduit through which your vibrations flow into the cards.

## STORING YOUR CARDS

Most readers also have methods and rituals for storing their Tarot decks. Many wrap their decks in silk, for silk is believed to possess special protective qualities that prevent the cards from becoming tainted by ambient energetic vibrations. You can use a silk scarf that has special meaning to you. Some people like to find a silk remnant from an older tradition, perhaps from an antique tapestry or a piece of cherished clothing such as a grandmother's wedding gown. You can simply fold your deck into the piece of cloth or make a pouch, either like an envelope or one with a drawstring.

<hr>

> Some Tarot enthusiasts insist that the cards should be kept in a pine box (as well as wrapped in silk) to keep bad vibrations from contaminating them. Care for your cards as you would any treasure or valued tool, but there's no need to get caught up in any rigid superstition about them.

<hr>

Some companies make beautiful velvet, satin, and tapestry pouches—with zippers or drawstrings—specially designed to hold Tarot cards. You could also store your deck in an attractive wooden box. Whatever you choose to store your cards in, keep your cards in a special, private place—you'll always know where they are when you want them and you can be sure they won't fall into the wrong hands.

# INTERPRETING THE TAROT

To learn how to read Tarot cards you must first familiarize yourself with your cards. As you study your cards, bear in mind that they have been derived from multiple cultures, and that behind them stands a mystery. Each person's reaction to the cards is as unique as a fingerprint. However, at first it is best to learn the standard interpretations. You can take off from there once you have studied and practiced with the cards. Learning to read the Tarot is like learning to play a musical instrument. It takes time, and the more effort you invest, the more proficient you will become.

# EXPLORING THE TAROT

A typical Tarot deck consists of seventy-eight cards. Of these, the first twenty-two are identified as the Major Arcana. The fifty-six remaining cards are called the Minor Arcana, presumably because they contain information that is of a less important or mystical nature. Because the Tarot can be viewed and understood as a body of wisdom and guidance, it is sometimes thought of as a book—or more accurately, as two books—of knowledge.

## THE MAJOR ARCANA

These arcana (which means "mysteries" or "secrets") represent the mysteries or secrets of the universe that reflect universal law. As such, they are the most complex cards in the deck and require more diligence to understand. Each of the Major Arcana cards, which are also called trump cards, is illustrated with specific symbols or scenarios, which are basically the same in all decks, even though they may differ thematically according to the philosophy of the designer. Each of the Major Arcana cards has a title, such as The Magician, The Empress, The Lovers, The Moon, The Tower, and so forth. They are numbered from zero—The Fool—to twenty-one—The World.

As seems to be the case in most schools of thought, particularly those that have been around for a while, there is disagreement about many aspects of the Major Arcana. Some scholars and authors focus primarily on the numerical order of the cards (zero to twenty-one) contending that they form a system through which the development of an individual's life can be traced. Some interpreters have interjected psychological meanings into the Major Arcana, while others have viewed them as a representative of spiritual development and growth.

## THE MINOR ARCANA

Most scholars agree that the Minor Arcana were added to the Major Arcana sometime in the fourteenth or fifteenth century. It is believed that this portion of the Tarot was originally used for fortune-telling, and that in earlier times, it was considered safe for nonadepts to have access to this part of the Tarot. The Minor Arcana consists of four suits of fourteen cards each: Wands, Pentacles, Swords, and Cups. Each suit contains four Court cards (King, Queen, Knight, and Page) and ten number cards from Ace through Ten, also called pip cards.

The Minor Arcana cards can be extremely accurate in answering questions about the here and now, as they refer to specific areas of everyday life and human experience. They do not describe spiritual growth per se, but can certainly be incorporated into a pattern of spiritual development. You don't need to search for some deep mystical meaning to attach to them, however.

To understand the Minor Arcana, it's important to realize that they serve as an adjunct to the Major Arcana—a sort of commentary within the context of the reading. This is not to imply that they have no real significance on their own, but rather that they are an integral part of the context of the entire reading. Their main function is to relate the readee (the person for whom the reading is being done) to the elements of the everyday world, which exist for all of us no matter how spiritual we are or how seriously we pursue a spiritual path.

Generally speaking, the cards of the Minor Arcana represent lesser, or mundane, lessons. They show the everyday concerns, situations, challenges, and achievements you experience in your personal life. As such, they also present advice and describe conditions and possibilities related to the subject of a reading.

The Minor Arcana may seem less important, but they provide immediate information. Through the study of the Minor Arcana, you can observe the ongoing process of how you grow and develop.

When many (or all) of the cards in a reading come from the Minor Arcana, it's safe to say your future is in your own hands. Your decisions and actions will produce your future. You have the ability to control your destiny.

# THE FOUR SUITS

In medieval times the four suits (usually called Wands, Pentacles, Swords, and Cups) represented the four main classes of people—the nobility, the clergy, the merchant class, and the working class. In today's society, there are correspondences—the elite, or old money, class is the nobility; today's version of the clergy has expanded to include the professions and academia; the merchant class includes businesses and people employed by corporate institutions; and those in blue-collar or service positions are the working class.

These suits help us pinpoint areas of life that need our attention, because each of the suits represents a distinct realm of activity, experience, and personal growth. When many cards of the same suit appear in a reading, it's a clear indication that the person consulting the Tarot is concerned about a particular area of life—or should be. A reading about a relationship will usually turn up several cards in the suit of Cups, whereas Pentacles are likely to predominate in a reading about finances. (See Part 2 for more information on the symbolism of the suits.)

## COURT CARDS

In most decks, each suit contains fourteen cards, including four Court cards. Usually these cards are called the King, Queen, Knight, and Page, although some designers use labels such as Knave, Prince, Princess, Lord, and Lady. The images on the Court cards are usually quite similar to those on ordinary playing cards—straightforward illustrations of a King, a Queen, a Knight, and a Page. Though there may be some variation in costume or colors, depending upon the philosophical orientation of the deck's creator, sometimes the only way to differentiate the suits is to note the symbol of the suit—Cup, Sword, Wand, or Pentacle—which is usually held by the person on the card.

The Court cards often represent actual people in the life of the individual for whom a reading is being done, or they may personify the readee. They can also be used as Significators. (Significators are discussed in further detail in the How to Do Readings chapter.)

In some cases, a King could represent a woman with the qualities of that particular King card. For example, the King of Pentacles could signify a strong, successful businesswoman. The Page cards can represent either sex, but they usually refer to a young person or a child who is involved in the experiences related to the suit to which the Page belongs. Pages can indicate messengers, students/apprentices, youths, or immature adults.

In addition to representing actual people in your life—family members, spouses or lovers, friends, coworkers, neighbors, and so on—the Court cards can symbolize influences in your environment. They can also refer to situations, conditions, or characteristics of the querent. Because our society today is more egalitarian than it was at the time the Tarot originated, it is possible to see a woman through a male card and vice versa. Here, feedback from the readee can help you to identify the person to whom a Court card is referring.

## THE NUMBERED CARDS

Each suit also includes an Ace, which is considered to be the One card, followed by cards numbered Two through Ten. Also known as pip cards, these combine the qualities of the suit with those of the number.

Interpretations of the Minor Arcana are likely to vary according to the worldview and intentions of the deck's designer. Some writers of books on the Tarot pay little attention to the Minor Arcana; others approach them mainly from the perspective of numerology. In many decks, the pip cards do not display any scenarios to suggest the card's meaning but merely show the corresponding number of the suit symbol. For example, the Three of Cups may simply depict three cups, without any storytelling imagery.

Although five hundred years' worth of Tarot students and masters have produced some agreement on the meanings of the Minor Arcana cards, there is also a good deal of disagreement, and sometimes the pictures on the cards tell a different story than would be indicated by the combination of number and suit. The Eight of Cups in the Waite deck, for example, shows a man walking away from eight cups, which suggests leaving a relationship or emotional situation behind. However, the number Eight connotes sincerity, abundance, and achievement, so drawing this card would suggest success in matters of the heart. Therefore, you may prefer to base interpretations of the pip cards on the number rather than on any particular illustration—unless, of course, your intuition hooks into the picture and it reveals something.

# TEACH YOURSELF TAROT

When you first begin the serious study of the Tarot, you may wish to spend the first hour of every day working with the cards. You can also learn the symbols and their meanings bit by bit as you practice laying out cards and interpreting them.

If you do not have the leisure to spend the first hour of the day with your cards, at least set aside some specific time, preferably daily, or as often as you can manage. Much will depend on your aims. If you merely want to do fortune-telling or predictions into the future, you can concentrate on the interpretations offered in this book and the chapters related to the spreads and readings. However, if you limit yourself to divination alone, you'll miss out on many of the benefits the Tarot can give you. Many people find the Tarot helps them to access psychological states and enhances their spiritual development.

### STEP ONE

If you decide to make a serious study of the Tarot to access its wisdom, begin by concentrating on each of the Major Arcana cards in turn. Begin with trump zero, The Fool. Read the description and the interpretation; compare the symbolism on the card to its counterpart in your deck (if you are not using the deck pictured in this book).

### STEP TWO

After you have familiarized yourself with the Major Arcana—the heart of the Tarot—turn to the Minor Arcana. Study the meanings of the four suits, for each suit corresponds to an area of life and represents a mode of interacting with the world. (You'll find interpretations of the individual cards of the Minor Arcana, arranged by suit, in Part 2.)

### STEP THREE

Next, move on to the Court cards: the Kings, Queens, Knights, and Pages. These cards often are used to represent people, although they have other meanings and purposes, too. Become familiar with the images on these cards and the distinctions between them.

### STEP FOUR

Last, examine the numbered cards of the Minor Arcana. When you have become familiar with all seventy-eight cards, you can begin to practice readings.

At first the task of remembering all seventy-eight cards may seem a bit overwhelming. But little by little, you'll find yourself growing more comfortable with the images, and you'll start to grasp the inherent system at work within the two books of the Tarot. Your intuitive responses will begin to make sense. You'll start to see connections between the cards that turn up in your daily sessions and what's going on in your life. Before long, you will find yourself gaining an appreciation of the breadth and depth of this time-honored source of wisdom that has fascinated some of the world's greatest minds for centuries.

## USE YOUR INTUITION

When you use the Tarot you are tapping your intuition. Your intuition, or sixth sense, is a valuable and often underutilized resource. In your unconscious, you have a huge data bank of experiences upon which to draw, most of which you are not even aware. As a result, you really know much more than you think you know. Your intuition has the unique ability to access knowledge and to correctly interpret the cards for you. In short, your unconscious is an innovator with great creative ability. Pay attention to it, trust it, let it guide you in your study of the Tarot—and in life.

∞∞∞∞∞∞∞∞∞∞∞∞∞∞∞∞∞∞∞∞∞∞∞∞∞∞∞∞∞∞∞∞∞∞∞∞∞∞∞∞∞∞∞∞∞∞∞∞

If at any time you feel uncomfortable while using the cards, stop and try again later. Pay attention to negative feelings. Make notes about any cards or symbols that produce anxiety or discomfort. Negative information is only that—information. Psychic information is like a weather forecast: If we know the weather is going to be stormy, we can take sensible precautions.

∞∞∞∞∞∞∞∞∞∞∞∞∞∞∞∞∞∞∞∞∞∞∞∞∞∞∞∞∞∞∞∞∞∞∞∞∞∞∞∞∞∞∞∞∞∞∞∞

## ACCESSING WISDOM

Symbolism is the language of the Tarot. Its symbols speak to a very deep, ancient part of you that is often ignored or discounted. By using the Tarot on a regular basis, you strengthen the connection between your ordinary, rational, mundane way of thinking and the other levels of existence—whether you view them as being inside or outside yourself. It's a bit like paying attention to your dreams. After a while, you'll start to understand things you didn't understand before.

When meditating on the cards or doing readings for yourself, you may get sudden, unexpected ideas or impressions that may—or may not—be directly related to a particular card or spread before you. These insights arise because working with the Tarot opens a portal between the selves (or between the different levels of reality) so that uninhibited communication can take place. Often these instantaneous revelations that slip in the back door of your mind are as meaningful as the reading itself. Sometimes, while you shuffle the cards, a single card will fall from the deck. Usually this card answers or sheds light on the question you're contemplating at the time. Is this just coincidence, or something akin to what C.G. Jung called synchronicity?

Like all oracles, and all intuitive tools, the Tarot lets you access wisdom in myriad ways. As you work with your deck, pay attention to all your experiences, your thoughts, feelings, impressions, and sensations. Like a good interpreter, the Tarot will enable you to communicate with parts of yourself that may have been shut off from you until now because you lacked an interface that would bring you together.

C.G. Jung was a Swiss psychologist who, in addition to studying with Sigmund Freud, made his own valuable contributions to psychology, including his theories about the unconscious. He coined the term "synchronicity" to describe the occurrence of meaningful events, that may appear to be simple coincidences but in fact are deeply related.

## WHERE TO BEGIN

Begin by examining the cards of the Major Arcana, the more important and complex cards in the deck, as they are considered to contain secret or spiritual knowledge. Carefully note each of the main figures on the cards—what they are doing, whether they are sitting or standing, their postures, the positions of their hands and limbs (what today is called body language), what they are looking at, etc. Pay attention to any other beings—human, animal, or spiritual—that appear with them. Some decks, including the Gilded Tarot and the Sacred Circle Tarot, incorporate animals, birds, insects, and reptiles into the cards' imagery to convey specific information. Notice also the background and the foreground, for each detail is an intentional and meaningful symbol. Even something that may seem minor, such as a flower or familiar household object, is a factor in the overall interpretation of the card. Then study the Minor Arcana in the same way.

Don't analyze your initial, immediate responses to the cards—just write down what comes to you spontaneously. If a question arises in your mind, write it down but don't try to answer it right away. Return to it later.

Make notes of your impressions—of the card as a whole and of individual symbols. Accustom yourself to noticing details and try to relate to the details on a personal level, asking yourself, "What does this mean to me?" For example, in the Waite deck, The Fool carries a rose. The rose has a generally accepted universal meaning, but your own interpretation might be different. Maybe roses hold a strictly personal meaning for you, based on your own life experience. Maybe you don't particularly care for roses. Maybe when you see a rose you think of the thorns instead of the fragrance. You can go with the standard interpretation, or substitute your own. As is true of dream symbols, your individual impressions are usually more significant than the commonly accepted ones.

⬦⬦⬦⬦⬦⬦⬦⬦⬦⬦⬦⬦⬦⬦⬦⬦⬦⬦⬦⬦⬦⬦⬦⬦⬦⬦⬦⬦⬦⬦⬦⬦⬦⬦⬦⬦⬦⬦

The natural inclination, for a beginner, is to interpret each card individually in a reading, and then to try to put together a whole picture from the individual pieces. But once you have impressed the meanings on your unconscious, you will find that a glance at an entire layout of cards will give you a picture of the totality. However, this only comes after much study and practice.

⬦⬦⬦⬦⬦⬦⬦⬦⬦⬦⬦⬦⬦⬦⬦⬦⬦⬦⬦⬦⬦⬦⬦⬦⬦⬦⬦⬦⬦⬦⬦⬦⬦⬦⬦⬦⬦⬦

Over time your impressions will change and expand. You may find that if you go back to a card after you've worked with the Tarot for a while you'll have a different slant on it. This means that the illustration has penetrated deeper into your unconscious. Remember that the cards are multilayered in meaning. What you derive from your initial examination of the pictures as well as the insights you glean over time will be important factors in how you understand and use the Tarot. Once you complete an intensive study of the Tarot, you'll be amazed at how significant your first impressions were to your entire process of learning to interpret.

# THE TAROT AS A TOOL FOR DIVINATION

The Tarot is a powerful tool, but it must be used properly and with respect, not only for the knowledge it contains but also for its ability to connect with the deepest recesses of the human psyche. Although the Tarot can be successfully used to answer mundane or practical questions, its highest value is as a guide to developing your intuition, which in turn leads to spiritual development.

Believe it or not, you already have the innate ability to get the answers you want. The Tarot, or any other physical tool, simply enables you to focus your intuition, the part of you that already knows the right answer. The Tarot cards are simply a convenient way to get at the inner truth of the situation.

Imagine this scenario: You need information about the future ramifications of a decision regarding a major life change. It could involve your career, your marriage, a relocation, a pregnancy, or someone close to you. Instead of worrying and wondering—or swinging back and forth between two alternatives—you simply take out your Tarot cards (or consult a professional reader).

Before using your cards, you take a few moments to relax completely according to your preferred method, slowly allowing your conscious mind to sink to the deep level of your inner unconscious mind. While holding your cards, or shuffling them, you formulate a succinct question about the situation for which you are seeking counsel. Calmly, you feel this question becoming a part of your entire being. Then you lay out your cards in a predetermined spread and voilà—the answer to your question is right there before you!

Sound impossible? It isn't. Right now you have this power. The problem is that you don't know you have it, and you don't know how to use it. But in fact your unconscious mind is already programmed to give you the answers you seek and need—once you know the correct keys to press to access the vast resources of information already in your mental software. That's where and why the Tarot can help.

## KEEP A TAROT JOURNAL

As you study the Tarot, it's a good idea to keep a journal. Use a bound notebook or three-ring binder with loose-leaf pages. At the top of each page write the name of a card. Each time you examine the card, date your entry. If you are doing readings, sketch the spread you've used and label each card. Add comments about your state of mind, situations in your life, or anything else that you feel may be relevant.

Once you have a journal devoted to your study of Tarot, make a covenant with your Tarot journal. Think for a few minutes about why you are doing this and why you are willing to make a commitment to writing your experiences—and copying your layouts, indicating what cards appear in which positions—regularly in your journal. Then put this into words. Study what you have written for a few minutes and see if you are satisfied with your purpose. You may want to make changes. Your statement of purpose might go something like this:

> *I'm keeping my Tarot journal for the purpose of getting in touch with my Higher Self, my intuition, and with the aim of generating heightened consciousness. My goal is to become more aware of messages from my sacred mind and to act on this information for my spiritual growth and development. I believe that keeping this journal will aid this process by providing me with a framework in which I can record and reflect upon my experiences and wherein I can chart my progress.*

You are making this agreement with yourself, and it is up to you to keep to the terms you make. Trust your inner self to keep up its part of the bargain.

# SYMBOLISM IN THE TAROT DECK

Individual Tarot decks express the themes that are important to their creators. Some decks express feminist sensibilities, while others depict Native American, Asian, or African motifs. Some, such as the Wheel of Change Tarot and the Universal Tarot, mix imagery from a variety of cultures and spiritual traditions. It is important that you are both aware of the symbols on your personal deck of cards and feel comfortable with them. Make friends with your cards and let them speak to you in terminology that is relevant to you. Every detail on each card—especially those in the Major Arcana—is a meaningful symbol. Symbols resonate on different levels of the psyche. One of the best ways to connect with these symbols is to contemplate and meditate upon those that are meaningful to you. How a card speaks to you and how you feel about the symbols it presents is what's important.

# SYMBOLS IN THE SUITS

Regardless of what spin a particular artist chooses to put on her deck, certain basic concepts will generally prevail. The four suits, for example, are fundamental to the Tarot's structure and composition. These suits correspond to the four elements, which are the building blocks of life, the vital and primal forces of the universe. These elements—Earth, Air, Fire, and Water—exist everywhere in our world, not only in a physical sense, but also as vibrations or energies. You can find them depicted not only in the Tarot but also in the four primary tools magicians use, the four directions, the four seasons, the Four Gospels in Christianity, and the Four Noble Truths in Buddhism.

Although the suit symbols are most evident on the Minor Arcana cards, they also appear in the Major Arcana. The Magician, for instance, is usually pictured with the symbols of all four suits before him, indicating his mastery of all the elements. The four suits may turn up on The World card, too, where they suggest a balance of these fundamental forces.

## WANDS

The suit of Wands corresponds to the element of Fire. Fire is active, outer-directed, linked with Spirit, will, self-expression, and inspiration. It suggests growth, expansion, and personal power. Because Fire represents archetypal masculine or yang energy, the symbolism used to depict this suit in the Tarot is distinctly phallic. Some decks use other images for the suit of Wands—rods, staves, clubs, branches sprouting leaves, lances, arrows, torches, or divining rods. Tarot of the Old Path shows them as brooms.

Often the people on the Wands cards (in storytelling decks) are shown as warriors, heroes, leaders, or magicians, dynamic and creative people who charge forth into life with confidence and enthusiasm. They may ride proud steeds, wave flags, or wear garlands. Whatever they are doing, they seem to be enjoying themselves. Even when they face challenges, as the Five and Ten cards frequently show, these courageous and hardy individuals seem fully capable of handling the difficulties placed before them and succeeding at whatever they undertake.

〰〰〰〰〰〰〰〰〰〰〰〰〰〰〰〰〰〰〰〰〰〰〰〰〰〰〰〰〰〰〰〰〰〰

You can find a Tarot deck to suit almost anyone's interests. The Baseball Tarot depicts Wands as—you guessed it—baseball bats. The Cooperstown Tarot depicts Cups as baseball gloves.

〰〰〰〰〰〰〰〰〰〰〰〰〰〰〰〰〰〰〰〰〰〰〰〰〰〰〰〰〰〰〰〰〰〰

When Wands appear in a spread or reading, it's usually an indication that some sort of action or growth is afoot. You might be embarking on an adventure of some kind or may be required to muster your courage in a challenging endeavor. Perhaps you could benefit from using your intuition instead of logic to solve a problem. Maybe you need to have fun, take some risks, assert yourself, or be creative.

## SWORDS

The suit of Swords relates to the element of Air. Like Fire, Air is a masculine/yang force, so its symbol, too, is obviously phallic. Although usually depicted as a mighty battle sword, the suit's symbol may be represented by ordinary knives, athames (ritual daggers used by magicians), scythes, axes, guns, or spears. Some swords are sturdy and functional; others are ornate, reminiscent of King Arthur's Excalibur. In the Wheel of Change deck, Swords are presented as shards of broken glass. However, the "weapon" represented by this suit is the intellect. As such, Swords symbolize rational thinking, logic, analysis, communication, and the power of the mind. The Child's Play Tarot uses pencils to denote the intellectual quality of this suit.

Storytelling decks frequently show the characters on the Swords cards as warriors, scholars, sages, teachers, or seekers, serious and dispassionate individuals who pursue answers to life's great questions. Often the images reveal suffering or strife, perhaps indicating the struggle involved in transforming experience into knowledge, or to illustrate the way in which Rudolf Steiner, on whose work the Waldorf Schools are founded, describes wisdom, which is as "crystallized pain."

The Nine and Ten of Swords, in particular, frequently depict painful scenes of worry, anxiety, and stress, which may be the result of too much thinking or relying too heavily on the intellect.

When Swords turn up in a reading, it often means that mental or verbal activity is a priority. Perhaps you are overworking your mind. Or you might need to use your head and examine an issue clearly and rationally. The King of Swords, for instance, can advise you not to let your heart rule your head. Swords also represent communication, study, or cutting through murky situations with logic and discrimination.

## CUPS

The suit of Cups is associated with the element of Water. Water's energy is receptive, inner-directed, reflective, connected with the emotions, creativity, and intuition. Because Water is a feminine or yin element, its symbols suggest the womb. In the Tarot, Cups are usually shown as chalices or goblets, but any type of vessel can depict the nature of the suit. Some decks picture them as bowls, cauldrons, vases, urns, flowers, pitchers, coffee mugs, steins, baskets, or bottles. Regardless of the imagery, the principle is the same—Cups represent the ability to receive and hold.

Because Cups represent water and its ability to be reflective and receptive, Cups can also describe a person who is intuitive, compassionate, sensitive, creative, or nurturing. All of these characteristics are traditionally feminine and relate to the inner reflections of a person and her emotional awareness.

For the most part, the scenes that appear on these cards suggest comfort, security, and contentment. Because the suit of Cups represents the emotions, the people on the cards are usually shown in relationships of some kind—romantic, familial, friendship. The Two of Cups symbolizes partnership, and frequently a man and woman appear together in a loving manner on the card. Three women friends often grace the Three of Cups, while the Ten of Cups depicts a happy home and family life.

A reading that contains many Cups usually emphasizes emotions and/or relationships. Depending on the cards involved, you may be enjoying positive interactions with people you care about or are seeking greater fulfillment in matters of the heart. Perhaps you are suffering a loss or disappointment, or are on your way to recovery and emotional renewal.

## PENTACLES

Pentacles or pentagrams (five-pointed stars) correspond to the Earth element. Like Water, Earth is a feminine/yin force that energetically relates to our planet as the source of sustenance, security, and stability. The suit of Pentacles represents practical matters, money and resources, the body, and the material world. Tarot decks often portray the suit as coins or discs, sometimes as shields, stones, rings, shells, crystals, wheels, stars, clocks, or loaves of bread. Regardless of the actual image used, the suit symbolizes physical resources, values, practical concerns, material goods, property, and forms of monetary exchange—things that sustain us on the earthly plane.

Storytelling decks often depict people on the Pentacles cards engaged in some form of work or commerce, or enjoying the fruits of their labors and the things money can buy. The Three of Pentacles in the Waite deck, for instance, shows a craftsman working at a forge. The Ten of Pentacles presents a picture of domestic security, abundance, and comfort. The Five of Pentacles, on the other hand, portrays a sad image of poverty and need.

When Pentacles appear in a spread, it's a sign that financial or work-related matters are prominent in the mind of the person for whom the reading is being done. In some cases, these cards can also signify physical or health issues, or other situations involving the body or one's physical capabilities. The Queen of Pentacles, for example, can indicate a sensual woman who is at home in her body, who loves good food, creature comforts, and the finer things in life. Depending on the cards, this suit may suggest a need to focus on practical concerns.

Or you could be too security-conscious and are putting emphasis on material things at the expense of spiritual, emotional, or intellectual considerations.

# THE POWER OF NUMBERS

The numbers on the pip cards of the Minor Arcana are of primary significance. Regardless of whether the deck you use includes storytelling images on these cards, pay attention to the number and the suit, for this combination provides the essential information in a reading.

Symbolically speaking, numbers are not merely arithmetic used to denote quantities. Each number also has a unique power and secret significance, applicable both to the spiritual and the material worlds. Numerology, the spiritual art of numbers, is thousands of years old. Cultures with an esoteric tradition have long honored and understood the sacred symbology of numbers. Numbers are indeed symbols and each possesses its own special characteristics. In fact, numbers could be considered our most common and familiar symbols.

When interpreting the number cards of the Minor Arcana, the suit will tell you the area of life to which the number card refers—the nature of the influences and forces at work and on which the specific number is commenting. By combining the meanings of the suit and the number featured on a card, you can determine how the card applies to the particular situation for which the reading is being given.

## ACE (ONE)

One signifies new beginnings. It implies something coming into being, the starting point of a whole new cycle. It represents self-development, creativity, action, progress, a new chance, a rebirth.

---

Barbara Moore, author of *The Gilded Tarot Companion*, calls Aces gifts from the universe. They symbolize a chance to start anew and realize possibilities and potential.

---

The Ace shows that a seed has been planted, meaning that something has begun, though you may not yet know how it will develop. The Aces symbolize potential growth. When an Ace appears in your reading, you are at a starting point, being offered a new opportunity. It's up to you to follow through—it won't automatically happen. The Ace indicates you have the choice to initiate something, that the time is ripe for new possibilities and growth.

The energy of One is solitary and self-contained. Drawing an Ace may indicate being alone or withdrawing into isolation to nurture a new idea, project, or experience before going public with it. Aces also can show focus, concentrated energy, and clarity of purpose.

## TWO

The essence of Two is duality. This number depicts some kind of union or partnership, with another person, a spiritual entity, or two parts of yourself. Two also represents the balance of polarities such as yin and yang, male and female, private and public, separate and together.

Two furthers the direction initiated with the Ace. It represents stabilizing and affirming the new opportunity. Sometimes Two shows a need to achieve balance with whatever new factor is being added to the situation that began with the Ace. Whether favorable or unfavorable, this addition will be of importance to you. Depending on the reading, the Two suggests either increased chances for a desirable outcome or greater obstacles involved in achieving that outcome.

Two's vibration can indicate sensitivity to others, perhaps to the point where you consider their needs over your own. "Two-ness" can also mean a state of immersing yourself in another person or in an idea or project.

## THREE

You see the essence of Three expressed in the trinity of Mind, Body, and Spirit. It is the number of self-expression and communication, of expansion, openness, optimism, and clarity.

With the Three, you begin to open up and see the big picture, understanding the details of how One and Two combine in your own process of growth and evolution. This is the point at which the project, idea, or relationship you initiated earlier now begins to take form. Three says "go," but if unfavorable factors are involved, caution is advised.

The number Three represents movement, action, growth, and development, but in some cases expansion can happen too fast. You may scatter your energies or spread yourself too thin. There is a tendency to leap before you look, or to buy now and pay later. However, properly handled, Three's vibration is cheerful, optimistic, and pleasant, representing a period of happiness and benefits, so long as you pay attention to what you are doing.

## FOUR

The number Four equates with foundation. There are four elements, four directions, and four seasons, so Four suggests totality, stability, and security. When Fours appear in a reading, it can indicate a time for self-discipline through work and service, productivity, organization, and pragmatism to establish a sound foundation.

Clarity is important now, so that you can work effectively to make your situation turn out positively. If you are in a place you want to be—a home, job, relationship—you might have to work to maintain stability; if you aren't where you want to be, drawing Fours suggests it's time to plan and work to make appropriate changes.

At this time, life can seem to be all work and no play, but sometimes that's necessary for you to accomplish your objectives. If your goals and purpose are clear, you won't mind doing the work, for you see the end result as beneficial. When Fours turn up in a reading, the message is to take slow, steady, determined steps and move patiently to bring your dreams to fruition.

## FIVE

Five is the number of freedom, instability, and change. Its vibration is active, physical, impulsive, impatient, resourceful, curious, and playful.

Drawing Fives in a reading suggests excitement, adventure, movement, and challenges afoot. It might even indicate a rollercoaster ride!

Sometimes, Five can be too much to handle, especially if you tend to be a quiet, sensitive person. The excitement and changes in your life may seem to be happening too fast, so that you feel you are caught in a whirlwind—or a hurricane. Thus Fives are often connected with stress and instability. You might need to slow down a bit and get some perspective before moving ahead. If an important decision is involved, "take five" before you make any commitment.

Although Fives are an indication to go for it, consider the risks involved, too. When Fives appear in a reading, you are willing to take risks because you love the excitement involved in the situation. The cards around the Five will indicate whether there is real danger or if things will work out to your advantage.

## SIX

Six is the number of service and social responsibility, caring, compassion, and community involvement. It signifies peace and quiet after the storm of Five. This is a time to keep it simple and attend to everyday needs, to rest, and to get into harmony with yourself and your surroundings. Any misunderstandings that occurred during an earlier period of upheaval can now be resolved harmoniously.

When Sixes appear in a reading, it's time to stop and catch your breath, realizing that you have created a comfortable pattern and can reap the rewards of your previous planning (Four) and risk-taking (Five). You feel centered and at ease with yourself and your circumstances. Unfavorable cards in the reading may indicate difficult circumstances yet to be faced, but Six cards rarely show anything negative themselves.

Six's vibration is cooperative; it can represent working with others or providing service of some kind. Just remember to take care of your own needs, too. In some cases, Sixes in a reading can show a tendency toward reclusiveness—just vegging out at home to enjoy a time of ease, especially after a period of intense activity or stress.

## SEVEN

The number Seven symbolizes the inner life, solitude, and soul-searching. Seven is a mystical number depicting wisdom and spirituality; there are seven heavens, seven days of the week (the seventh being holy), seven colors in the visible spectrum, seven notes in a musical scale, and seven major chakras.

When Sevens appear in a reading, it indicates a time of turning inward to discover the meaning of life, what has been happening to you, and why. You may be searching, on a psychological or spiritual level, for answers. Perhaps you feel an intense need to be alone. Seven often refers to birth and rebirth, religious inclinations, and spiritual resources. Some people retreat from the busyness of everyday life at this time, take vows of some kind, or begin to practice ritual as part of their inner development. Emblematic of the path of solitude, analysis, and contemplation, Seven marks a time when you are exploring your own individuality in your own way.

This is not a time to begin projects related to the material or financial world. Your energy is focused on the inner rather than the outer realm. Now is a good time to create a sanctuary for contemplation, a private place where you can examine your past experiences and evaluate the present. You might wish to study or research metaphysical subjects, start paying attention to dreams and ESP experiences—whatever will help you to find your own true path in life. In some cases, Sevens in the reading may indicate that you are spending too much time alone and need to socialize.

## EIGHT

Eight represents abundance, material prosperity, and worldly power or influence. It is the number of leadership and authority. On the spiritual level, Eight symbolizes cosmic consciousness; infinity's symbol is a figure Eight turned on its side. This powerful number indicates you possess the organizational and managerial skills that contribute to material success—or that you need to develop them. If you have been devoting much of your time and energy to spiritual progress, the appearance of Eights in a reading indicates it's time to get your financial or worldly affairs in order.

⸎⸎⸎⸎⸎⸎⸎⸎⸎⸎⸎⸎⸎⸎⸎⸎⸎⸎⸎⸎⸎⸎⸎⸎⸎⸎⸎⸎⸎⸎⸎⸎⸎⸎⸎⸎⸎⸎⸎⸎⸎⸎⸎⸎

> As the infinity glyph symbolizes wholeness, the number Eight points to the development of multiple aspects of your life—physical, mental, and spiritual.

⸎⸎⸎⸎⸎⸎⸎⸎⸎⸎⸎⸎⸎⸎⸎⸎⸎⸎⸎⸎⸎⸎⸎⸎⸎⸎⸎⸎⸎⸎⸎⸎⸎⸎⸎⸎⸎⸎⸎⸎⸎⸎⸎⸎

Eight's vibration is linked with honor, respect, equality, awards, public recognition, power, and abundance in all areas of life. When you draw Eights, the potential for achieving these benefits is likely, but sincerity and dedication are needed.

The Eight cards also caution you to consider the welfare of others as well as yourself. If there are unfavorable factors in the reading, you may need to be careful with money or possessions. Eights reversed can indicate that you have many issues around abundance—or the lack of it—yet to resolve.

## NINE

The number Nine equates with humanitarianism. It represents universal compassion, tolerance for the many differences among different peoples, and the attainment of wisdom through experience. Drawing Nines suggests you have reached a level where you are comfortable dedicating your life to others' welfare, or to some worthy cause. The challenge is to avoid getting so caught up in the big picture—the greatest good for the greatest number—that you neglect what is closest to you.

Nine symbolizes integration and, in a reading, shows that you have established your life priorities—you know what you want and how you intend to get it. You feel a flow of vitality between all the different parts of yourself. You understand the interaction between you and the world as a continuing process of living, being, moving. The Nine vibration allows you to see beyond the boundaries of the self into the totality of the universal. You are able to give freely of yourself because you feel complete within yourself.

The last single-digit number, Nine represents the end of a cycle. It's time to tie up loose ends. In most cases, the Nine cards depict fulfillment, completion, wholeness, and the sense of satisfaction that comes from having reached a peak after a long, arduous climb.

## TEN

Ten represents both an ending and a beginning, the point of transition from the completed cycle to the new cycle, which has not yet manifested. When Tens show up in a reading, whatever you have been working on or involved with is over. You've got whatever you are going to get out of it, and now it is time to bring in the new cycle that's been waiting in the wings.

Whether the cycle that's ending has been good or bad, you know it's over now, which is especially gratifying if you have been experiencing rocky times. If you have become complacent during a good period, drawing Tens tells you the time has come to challenge yourself and reach for a higher level. As a compound number, Ten, though a form of One, has more impact and therefore adds an extra dimension in a reading. Like ascending to a higher level of a spiral staircase, you can look down at precisely where you began and chart your progress. Now you have a choice to either stagnate in familiar and comfortable territory or to take a chance and start something new and different.

As happens in any period of transition, you may experience discomfort about making the decision to stay put or move on. Both options are available; both require thought and consideration. You might feel you are sitting on the fence, with one foot on either side, not sure whether to jump all the way over. Transitions are like that, and sometimes it takes quite a while to get both feet on the same side of the fence. However, you know that "he who hesitates is lost," and though you have the luxury of postponing both decision and action for a little while, when Tens show up in a reading it's a signal that a decision must be made.

## THE MEANING OF COLOR

Many Tarot decks display vivid and beautiful color palettes. But the colors shown on the cards are not purely decorative; they embody specific symbolic, spiritual, psychological, and physiological properties as well. For centuries, artists have used colors in their compositions, not only for their aesthetic properties, but also for their ability to convey moods and messages to those who view them.

In magical practice, colors correspond to the four elements. Red is associated with Fire, blue with Water, green with Earth, and yellow with Air. Because each suit is linked with an element, many Tarot artists use the colors connected with the corresponding suits to trigger subconscious responses and insights. Therefore, some decks emphasize red on the cards in the suit of Wands, blue on the Cups cards, green on the Pentacles cards, and yellow on the Swords cards.

Early Christian paintings and stained glass windows often show Jesus and Mary dressed in blue robes, which suggest serenity and compassion. We connect orange with fire, the sun, and warmth, while green represents growth, health, and in some countries, money.

Studies show that people react psychologically and even physically to colors. For instance, red tends to make us feel stimulated, warmer, and can even raise your pulse rate and body temperature slightly. Blue, conversely, calms and cools us. In some prisons, cell walls were painted pink and aggressive behavior among inmates declined. The following table lists qualities associated with different hues. As you familiarize yourself with your Tarot deck, notice how the artist has used colors to express certain qualities.

| COLOR | INTENTION |
| --- | --- |
| Red | Passion, vitality, courage |
| Orange | Warmth, energy, activity, drive, confidence |
| Yellow | Creativity, optimism, enthusiasm |
| Green | Healing, growth, fertility, prosperity |
| Light blue | Purity, serenity, mental clarity, compassion |
| Royal blue | Loyalty, insight, inspiration, independence |
| Indigo | Intuition, focus, stability |
| Purple | Wisdom, spirituality, power |
| White | Purity, wholeness, protection |
| Black | Power, the unconscious, banishing, wisdom |
| Pink | Love, friendship, affection, joy, self-esteem |
| Brown | Grounding, permanence, practicality |

## FAMILIAR SYMBOLS

In addition to the suit symbols, you'll find many familiar—and some not so familiar—images on the cards in your deck. Tarot artists intentionally choose symbols from various spiritual, cultural, magical, and psychological traditions to convey information directly to your subconscious. Like dream imagery, the symbols depicted on Tarot cards speak to people at a deep level and trigger insights in a way that's more immediate and succinct than words can.

Symbols and pictures offer other advantages over words, too. Because images are understood by our inner knowing, they are less likely to present you with dogma when you seek truth. They inspire you to think, but they don't tell you what to think. They bypass the analytical, orderly left-brain and strike up a lively conversation with the imaginative, flexible right-brain. Like myths, symbols transcend the boundaries of religion, nationality, and time, presenting universal themes and concepts that people everywhere can relate to.

The cards in the Major Arcana, in particular, are rich with meaningful imagery, although many decks include vivid symbolism on the Minor Arcana cards as well. Some of the symbols are universal in nature, found in many countries and time periods. Others are personal and may reflect the designer's intentions or beliefs, rather than holding broader meanings for all users. The Universal Tarot, by Maxwell Miller, incorporates a variety of symbolism from many different traditions to create a complex and comprehensive oracle.

## UNIVERSAL SYMBOLS

Symbols embody the essence of whatever they stand for; they aren't merely a convenient form of shorthand. That's why they have such power, why they appear in diverse and widely separated cultures, and why they have endured for millennia.

---

Symbol is myth's vehicle, the chariot by which legend and story, and myth's higher form, religion, are drawn through the heart and mind, and through time. Symbols express underlying patterns of thought and feeling stemming from the mythological roots that still affect people in a very real way.

---

Symbols that turn up again and again, in all parts of the world, possess universal appeal and resonate in what Swiss psychiatrist C.G. Jung called the collective unconscious. They mean essentially the same thing to everyone, regardless of age, race, religion, or nationality and get around the limitations of the rational, analytical left-brain. Often you may confront these symbols in dreams where they provide guidance and awaken you to parts of yourself that you may have ignored in your waking life. The Tarot works in a similar manner.

The following table shows a number of common, universally understood symbols that you may notice on the cards in your Tarot deck. They can be helpful keys as you examine the cards and learn their significances.

| SYMBOL | MEANING |
|---|---|
| Circle | Wholeness, unity, protection, continuity |
| Square | Stability, equality, structure |
| Triangle | Trinity, three-dimensional existence, movement |
| Downward triangle | Divine feminine, Earth or Water elements |
| Upward triangle | Divine masculine, Fire or Air elements |
| Star | Hope, promise |
| Five-pointed star | Protection, the human body, physical incarnation |
| Six-pointed star | Union of male/female or earth/sky, integration, manifestation |
| Vertical line | Movement, heaven, sky, masculine energy |
| Horizontal line | Stability, earth, feminine energy |
| Cross | Union of male/female or earth/sky, integration, manifestation |
| Spiral | Life energy, renewal, movement toward the center |
| Sun | Clarity, vitality, optimism, contentment, masculine energy |
| Moon | Secrets, intuition, emotions, feminine energy |
| Dove | Peace, reconciliation, promise |
| Crane | Wisdom |
| Rose | Love |

| SYMBOL | MEANING |
| --- | --- |
| Mountain | Challenge, vision, achievement |
| Ocean/water | Emotions, the unknown depths of the psyche |
| Snake | Transformation, hidden knowledge, kundalini energy |
| Egg | Birth, fertility |
| Rainbow | Renewal, hope, happiness |
| Book | Knowledge |
| Lantern | Guidance, clarity, hope |
| Bridge | Connection, harmony, overcoming difficulty |
| Tree | Knowledge, growth, protection, strength |
| Butterfly | Transformation |

When studying the symbolism in the Tarot, remember that your own responses and interpretations are what count most. Cars suggest movement and freedom to most people, but if you were in a serious auto accident when you were young, cars may represent pain or danger to you. Trust your own instincts and intuition. After all, your Tarot deck and your subconscious are attempting to communicate with you, and they will do it in imagery that you can understand.

## PERSONAL SYMBOLS

Tarot decks can also contain their creators' personal symbols. These images may or may not mean the same thing to you as they do to their designers or to another person using the cards. Flexibility is part of what makes the Tarot so fascinating.

Perhaps the artist is attempting to get you to stretch your imagination by presenting you with new or atypical pictures. The noted and eclectic artist Salvador Dalí repeats individual symbols such as a forked stick on some of the cards in his deck, as well as omitting or altering some familiar imagery entirely. The World card in his deck is anything but a pretty picture of joy, harmony, and abundance—possibly because the artist views our world as disturbing and never completely fathomable.

Tarot decks that come packaged with their own books or instructional guides generally explain the significance of the symbols displayed on the cards. Even so, if your own feelings about the pictures on the cards don't coincide with the artist's, give your own responses precedence. And if your interpretations of certain symbols change over time, that's okay, too.

### PART 2

# THE MAJOR AND MINOR ARCANA

# MEANINGS OF THE MAJOR ARCANA

It would be hard to find a more appropriate tool for spiritual and personal growth than the Major Arcana. For centuries, seekers have used this body of occult wisdom to access hidden knowledge and to connect with the higher realms. These powerful images portray archetypes that exist within the collective unconscious and that connect you to something larger than yourself. At the spiritual level, each of the Major Arcana cards represents a state of being, or an inner truth about yourself. This chapter will examine each of the trumps individually to understand their symbols and the meanings of specific cards when they appear in a reading.

# INTRODUCTION TO THE TRUMPS

The cards in the Major Arcana represent forces beyond yourself and the limits of mundane, earthly, human existence. Depending on your personal worldview, you could think of these forces as fate, god, goddess, cosmic, karma, or your own Higher Self. Whichever way you choose to see the energies or entities behind the cards, they indicate that something larger, outside yourself is influencing you and the issue about which you are seeking advice.

The simplest way to understand the Major Arcana in spiritual terms is to think of it as an ascending staircase with twenty-two steps. Each card represents a lesson you must learn in order to move up to the next step. And you have to figure out how to do this yourself; there is no set system.

When many trumps turn up in a reading, it's a signal that the situation is not entirely in your own hands or that you are not alone in the matter that concerns you. Higher forces outside your control may be at work, perhaps guiding the outcome. Because these cards can be linked with archetypes, they may portray dimensions of greater significance that are influencing your situation.

A reading that contains more cards from the Major Arcana than from the Minor Arcana suggests that you may not have a great deal of choice in how the issue turns out. You might not be able to control what happens. In some cases, a predominance of trump cards shows that previous actions or decisions have set things in motion, and now you are being propelled toward the inevitable result.

## STUDYING THE TRUMPS

You can either study the trump cards in consecutive order, or choose individual cards that represent areas or concepts you wish to work on, in whatever order suits your purposes. Or separate the Major Arcana from the entire deck, shuffle, and draw a card for study, letting your inner knowing guide you.

If, for example, you wish to discover the source of inner strength, pick the Strength card. Start by simply gazing at the card, without analyzing it. Let the colors, pictures, and symbols connect with your intuition and reveal themselves to you gradually, before you begin to examine the images more carefully.

The Major Arcana cards possess many different layers. As you work with them, these layers reveal themselves. It's a bit like digging into an archeological site. For example, on a strictly practical level, The Empress may be a direct reference to your mother or your desire to become a mother. On the mundane level, The Magician may refer to your desire to live a more creative life, to be more creative in your work. On the level of spiritual development, The Devil may indicate that it is time for you to throw off the obstacles that are preventing your living more fully and deeply, that you should tend to your soul needs rather than your material concerns.

Each individual unfolds according to his or her own inner blueprint. There's no hurrying the process, which ultimately takes place on its own time schedule. The cycles in life show you the patterns you are following and suggest new directions. The Major Arcana can be a guide that helps you to explore universal concepts as they apply to your life at any given moment.

## DESCRIPTION

The Fool is a fascinating figure, yet he can be an ambiguous symbol. Related to the jester or the joker of the ordinary playing deck, which is often used as the wild card, he seems beyond ordinary cares and concerns.

In the Waite deck, The Fool is shown as a male figure standing on the edge of a cliff, as if about to step off into thin air, yet his gaze is brightly upward as if he expects the heavens to support him. In some decks, he is looking back over his shoulder, but he is always unconcerned—or unaware— of any danger lying ahead. Usually The Fool is youthful, but sometimes he is an

THE FOOL.

older traveler who has obviously been on the road a long time.

Like a hobo, he carries all his worldly possessions tied in a small bag on a stick over his shoulder. Behind him, the sun, symbol of the source of all life, is shining on his enterprise.

He may carry a rose, symbol of love, or a traveler's staff. Often he is dressed in bright colors, and the card's general impression is cheerful and sunny. Sometimes he is wearing the parti-colored costume and cap and bells of a medieval court jester, or he might be dressed in the plain garb of a wanderer.

Often he is accompanied by a dog, which is a symbol of your natural instincts, for a dog has the uncanny ability to follow an invisible trail, using his nose and other senses. The little dog gambols about The Fool, sometimes pulling him back from the danger ahead, suggesting that our instincts, if followed, do provide us with guidance on our life journeys.

Ordinarily, The Fool is shown as a person full of confidence—often the confidence of youth—and trust in the beneficence of the universe.

He symbolizes that blind leap of faith that we all must take upon entering the journey of life itself, especially if that journey is spiritual.

## INTERPRETATION

When The Fool appears in a reading, depending on its position in the layout, it symbolizes someone who is about to embark on a new way of life. This may involve a physical journey, moving to a new place, starting a new job, or getting married or divorced. Often, the appearance of The Fool indicates a person who is ready to start on a spiritual path, who has made peace with the need to experience absolute faith and trust in the universe. In such a case, the person has no sense of worry or fear and feels that she is protected and that everything will turn out well. The person may be consciously in touch with the intuitive realm of her being, or she may simply be naive about what the future will bring. The Fool represents a state of openness and faith that she'll be supported in her adventure.

## UPRIGHT

At this time, you are out of sync with the rest of the world, but in a positive way. You may want to go out on your own, "Full speed ahead and damn the torpedoes." Or you may feel somehow isolated from the general group, a loner. Your experience of the current situation is different from those around you, which may make you feel as if you are marching to a different drummer, and you probably are. You need to listen to that different drummer, for this is the beat of your authentic self trying to get your attention.

## REVERSED

The time for independent action may not be right. You must discriminate between your personal fantasies—of going off on an adventure or chucking it all for a new track—and reality. The advice given to people who want to become writers or artists may apply here: "Don't quit your day job." This is not to say that what you want to do is invalid, only that you must consider all of the pros and cons carefully.

## DESCRIPTION

The Magician is powerful, representing worldly wisdom and the control of unseen forces that operate in human lives. A deeply complex symbol, he is usually depicted as a male figure who stands alone before an array of the traditional magician's tools. In most decks, these are the symbols of the Minor Arcana suits, each of which corresponds to one of the four elements: a pentacle for Earth, a sword for Air, a cup for Water, and a wand for Fire. To possess knowledge of these elements is to gain mastery in the world.

In the Waite deck, The Magician holds a wand, a phallic symbol, aloft in

THE MAGICIAN.

one hand toward the heavens, or the upper world of divine power, while his other hand points downward to the earth, the base of life. Above his head floats the symbol for infinity. He knows how to use his tools to connect the two worlds of spirituality, or metaphysics, and physicality, or the mundane plane of existence.

In the Waite deck, above him are trailing vines, like grapes, symbol of wine, a sacred drink in many cultures. At his feet is a garden of roses, lilies, and greenery. These represent the vegetable kingdom in general. Roses refer to desire and the five senses; lilies refer to purity and proper use of arcane knowledge.

The totality of these symbols tells us that The Magician is in possession of knowledge that enables him to manipulate the material world through aligning it with the spiritual plane, to create the desired circumstances.

## INTERPRETATION

The appearance of The Magician in a reading indicates latent powers, yet to be taken up and brought into manifestation. Also known as The Juggler, this card suggests that everything in the universe is spread out before us, and if we learn to use them correctly we can manifest the results we desire. These are literally the basic materials of creation, and it is the task of The Magician to handle them well, to manipulate and control them for beneficent purposes. This is mental work that affects the material realm.

Thus, The Magician shows us that what we consider to be illusion is another form of reality, and what we consider to be reality can be mere illusion. This is not trickery, but a deep understanding of how we must learn to use our intellects, our intuitive abilities, our personal talents, and our practical skills to mediate between the two worlds, both of which affect us simultaneously.

The Magician is a card of power, for just as a mage, or true magician, stands at the center of the universe with the tools and ability to manipulate it for his purposes, so does each of us create, or re-create, our own universes within ourselves, first in our minds, and then in our manifest realities. This card tells us that our nature is one with the nature of the universe. It suggests that we have the ability to control our own lives, that we can manipulate people, things, and events—so long as we go about it the right way and for the right ends.

The Magician's costume varies with different decks—from Egyptian to Greek to medieval—but he usually wears a belt. In the Waite deck, this is a coiled snake, the ouroboros, or snake biting his tail, an alchemical symbol for wholeness. This represents the power to heal through connecting the two worlds within one's self.

This card is primarily about self-development; as Tarot Arcanum One, it is the beginning of the road to spiritual enlightenment, the starting point. It does not say that we are already able to control our universes, but that we must learn what mode to use to gain our ends and reach our goals, whether they are spiritual or mundane.

The Magician suggests the use of higher intuitive forces, which may appear as a flash of insight. The Magician can serve as an inner guide who, if we listen carefully, will prompt us to develop and fulfill our potential—from within.

## UPRIGHT

This is a situation of new beginnings and new choices. It indicates someone who is willing and able to manipulate the situation to achieve the desired ends. It suggests leadership potential, ambition, desire for action, and new relationships coming into being. The tools for whatever action you desire are already at hand, as is the knowledge for using them correctly. It is a time to evaluate the tools you have at your disposal and relate them properly to your aims.

## REVERSED

Now is not the time for change. It may be that you are not ready internally, or that you are not fully prepared in an external way. New directions are in the making, but patience is required for them to work out properly. You may be experiencing self-doubt about a new venture, or your spirits and vitality may be too low to accomplish the action required. Creativity abides in the latent stage, like a caterpillar in its cocoon, and there is no sense in rushing things prematurely. Wait until the time is ripe.

# THE HIGH PRIESTESS

## DESCRIPTION

The High Priestess is a most mysterious card, representing that which has yet to be revealed, secret knowledge, the duality of life on earth. She symbolizes feminine spiritual power, or the goddess from whom all life comes and to whom all returns in the ever-cycling round of earthly existence.

She is depicted as a serene-faced female figure, sometimes seated with a book on her lap. In the Waite deck, this book bears the word "Torah," but in other decks it is merely an open book or scroll suggesting the divine law that underlies the manifest universe. The scroll or book represents the Akashic Records, the divine repository of our lives past, present, and future. Sometimes, she is standing, holding a staff and pointing toward an unseen object in the distance, another indication of something yet to be revealed.

THE HIGH PRIESTESS.

She sometimes sits or stands between two pillars, which represent the opposites of the dual nature of our world: good and evil, light and dark, truth and deception, positive and negative. She promises reconciliation of these opposites to those willing to follow the spiritual path of understanding universal law. In the Waite deck, The High Priestess sits at the doorway to the temple, which symbolizes the body, as if welcoming students to enter and learn her secrets. However, the crescent moon at her feet warns of the danger of releasing higher knowledge to those unprepared to handle it.

In the Waite deck, two pillars represent a doorway to the interior of life's mysteries, with The High Priestess as the guardian of the entryway. Also in the Waite deck, she sits against a background of pomegranates, a reference to Persephone, daughter of Demeter, who leaves the daylight, or upper world, for six months each year to tend to the dead in the underworld. In some decks, she carries flowers or is depicted against a background of vegetables and vegetation, another reference to the goddess, or Grain Mother.

On her breast, The High Priestess wears a cross, symbolic of the four elements—Fire, Earth, Air, and Water—held in balance. She wears a crown, usually a crescent, the horns of the moon, or a variant of it. In the Waite deck, between the horns sits a sphere, representative of the full moon, while the horns echo the images of the waxing and waning moon. The three lunar phases symbolize the three stages of womanhood: maiden, mother, crone.

## INTERPRETATION

When The High Priestess appears, she indicates that something hidden, or interior, is preparing to come forth or that the person needs to pay more attention to his inner world of dreams, imagination, and intuition. She advises him to develop awareness of the totality of himself, the night side, so to speak, as well as the daylight personality and activities. Usually, the person is ready to accept the importance of developing this part of his life but may have been holding back out of fear or inertia.

The High Priestess may indicate that the person is attempting to hide something that needs to be revealed. Or she can mean that the person is too much involved in an isolated inner world and needs to reconcile the inner life with the outer one.

Psychologically, the underworld refers to the unconscious, or what is in the process of coming into being. In this twilight realm, of which dreams are a component, we encounter our inner selves through intuition and fantasy. The High Priestess is an image representing our potentials that have yet to be discovered and brought forth—our secret selves longing to be recognized.

## UPRIGHT

You are experiencing a high degree of awareness of the invisible world, where inner change takes place before it manifests in the outer, material world. Your attunement to these inner, invisible sources is acute now, and you are in a position to take advantage of this fact. You may want to remove yourself, literally, from your day-to-day life to go deeper into your inner core. Tune in to your inner voice and spiritual awareness.

## REVERSED

Something within you is seeking greater recognition of your inner needs, which you may have been neglecting, although at a deep level you are aware that something is stirring. You may be tuning in to yourself in a very private way, not wanting others to know about this activity. Those around you may notice that you seem vague, or not quite yourself, and you may be fending off comments about your not being here. Ignore them. You are in the process of finding your own personal way into your inner world and the riches it contains.

## DESCRIPTION

The Empress is a card of beauty and creativity, the matriarch incarnate, symbolic of the Universal Mother as monarch. She represents the social concept of the feminine in the maternal role: procreation, nurturing, the security and comforts of home, and domestic harmony.

The Empress is always a mature female figure, often seated on a throne. In some decks, she is standing in a field, surrounded by flowers and vegetation representative of the bounty of Mother Nature and her harvest. Full-breasted and sometimes pregnant, she symbolizes fruitfulness and earthly abundance. As a symbol of The Empress's royal

THE EMPRESS.

position, she sometimes holds a scepter and wears an imperial crown of great magnificence. In many decks, a shield or coat of arms leans against her throne, at her feet. In the Waite deck, this is heart-shaped and bears the astrological symbol for Venus. Venus is the planet of love, beauty, desires, and pleasure—the quintessential traditional feminine symbol.

## INTERPRETATION

When The Empress appears, a strong feminine energy is at work. As a mother figure and representative of the traditional female role, The Empress is a creative force that works for harmony. She brings disparate things together, reconciling differences, like a mother running a household must do. This is a card of emotional control and making things work congenially toward a common social goal.

The Empress also refers to the person's emotional and physical resources—for nurturing, healing, feeding, and supporting other people. Often, there is a situation in the person's life where love and nurturing are required—sometimes by the person herself, sometimes by others in the environment. This card is related to the caretaking process and may refer to the way the person was mothered, for the first and most significant relationship you form is with your mother, and this relationship has a direct bearing on all subsequent relationships. Sometimes The Empress indicates that the person either had an overbearing "smother mother," or is acting out that role.

As a female authority, The Empress's appearance may signify, depending on its place in the spread, the person's need to become that female authority, especially if the person is a woman. In a man's reading, the indication is that he needs to recognize the feminine component of himself and acknowledge its power to unite opposing forces.

## UPRIGHT

You are in a position of nurturing someone else, or several others. This could be caring for children or the sick or being supportive of a spouse or friend in need. This card could also refer to a pregnancy, or the desire for a pregnancy. It is appropriate for you to be nurturing now, for you have the inner strength and the ability to do so without harming or depleting yourself.

## REVERSED

This is a time for you to be nurturing yourself. You may have been spending too much time caring for others (or you may have recently had a child whose demands have worn you out). This is an indication that you need to take time out for yourself instead of neglecting your own personal needs. This is a call for self-love and the awareness that you deserve the same care and attention you give to your loved ones. Maintain a balance between the needs of others and your own, equally valid needs.

## DESCRIPTION

The Emperor is a figure of supreme authority, as his title suggests. He is usually shown seated on a throne, sometimes flanked by animals. In the Waite deck, these are ram's heads, symbolic of masculine power. He wears robes over a full suit of armor, holds a scepter in the shape of the Egyptian ankh, and is crowned elaborately. In some decks, his shield, bearing the symbol of the imperial eagle, leans against the throne. He is clearly a figure to be reckoned with. Often he appears outdoors, against a backdrop of mountains, another reference to worldly power. His age and position of authority speak of experience and wisdom gained. Although he is depicted as a warrior, his attitude is one of kindness as the beneficent ruler of his empire.

THE EMPEROR.

While at rest, The Emperor's attitude suggests he is willing to fight for what is right and what is his duty to protect. He is the executive, or leader, who has reached the summit of authority and achieved worldly power.

Thus, The Emperor is a father figure, as The Empress is a mother figure. He lays down the ideals, morals, and aspirations for the entire family to follow. He is the builder in the material world who strives to make constructions of lasting value and importance.

## INTERPRETATION

When The Emperor appears in a reading, look for issues related to authority. Although The Emperor represents worldly power and wisdom, he is not simply a figure who gives commands to others. His achievement is to understand that peace and security require a willingness and ability to defend it. "The price of freedom is eternal vigilance."

---

The Emperor is related to Zeus, the father-god of the Greek pantheon. The Romans called him Jupiter; the Norse called him Thor. All these deities were known for throwing thunderbolts, or lightning. In some decks The Emperor carries lightning instead of the ankh.

---

The Emperor is a teacher figure, and what he teaches is the meaning of power and how to use it in this world. Though not overtly aggressive, he tells us that it is necessary sometimes to take up arms against evil forces. With The Emperor, there is no waffling about what is right and good, no rationalizing that the ends justify the means. As a protective male force, especially of the home and of domestic harmony, he personifies the ideal that what is worth having is worth fighting for.

The Emperor in a reading can also indicate issues concerning one's biological father, or authority figures. He can show that the time has arrived to become the authority figure, rather than depending on others to provide protection. The Emperor often appears when the person is struggling to achieve personal independence, to overcome the inner parent tapes, to become his own person. The Emperor says that one must, often late in life, come to terms with what "father" means, and reconcile related issues.

When The Emperor appears, he can be an indication that the individual's real father has either recently died or may die soon, a situation that can bring up feelings of being abandoned by a protective father figure. Even if the personal father was a negative factor, there is always a yearning for someone else to take care of us, protect us, and advise us. It is important to remember though that separation from the parents is a crucial stage in human development and must be accomplished. It's also possible that someone in the person's life is acting as a father figure, perhaps a boss or a husband. Whether this is positive or negative will be indicated by the placement of the card in the layout.

## UPRIGHT

This is an indication that you are involved with the established order, or with someone who represents the establishment. You may have a need to identify with a powerful group, whether religious, ideological, intellectual, economic, or political—to be one of them. Or you may be associating with someone else who has this need.

## REVERSED

You may be in conflict with the established order—perhaps at your job or with your family, religion, or ethnic group. Perhaps you feel pressured to accept responsibilities you don't want, or don't feel capable of handling. You may have recently experienced a loss of power, such as through downsizing, or you may lack the energy required to reach your goals. A need for more experience, drive, or improved health could be indicated.

# THE HIEROPHANT

## DESCRIPTION

The Hierophant is a figure with authority and power, like The Emperor, but The Hierophant's power is of a spiritual nature whereas The Emperor's is temporal. Often, he is shown as a religious leader, such as the Pope of Roman Catholicism. Some decks title him The Pope. He is usually seen seated on a throne, dressed in priestly raiment, crowned, and holding a scepter. His implements will vary according to the religious theme of the deck.

His scepter symbolizes the three worlds—the physical, the astral, and the etheric. His free hand is held aloft in a position of blessing. Two or three

**THE HIEROPHANT.**

acolytes may stand before him, either as participants, supplicants, or students, deferring to his wisdom and understanding him as a representative of religious authority.

Like The Emperor, he contains within himself the wisdom of a spiritual calling, and like The High Priestess, The Hierophant frequently sits or stands between two pillars, which signify the duality of matter and spirit.

In this role, The Hierophant can be seen as a teacher to those who seek the keys to the sacred Mysteries. The Waite deck shows two crossed keys below him, representing the intellect and intuition and the need to use them in tandem. He is responsible for making spiritual decisions for others and for blessing them. Unlike The High Priestess, whose world is primarily internal and ephemeral, The Hierophant's influence is of this world, and his spirituality can be achieved through conscious choices made on an intellectual basis.

## INTERPRETATION

The Hierophant suggests that the person has chosen a religion or philosophy with which to guide his or her life. In such a case, there is usually a great deal of loyalty to it, whatever the person's concept of god may be. Sometimes the card indicates disentangling yourself from such an association.

In some organized religions, the supreme deity does not speak to the individual directly, or to the general populace. Therefore, institutionalized religion makes use of human interpreters who convey the word of god (the divine will) to their followers.

The Hierophant symbolizes any organized institution—be it religious, philosophical, educational, spiritual, or temporal—that exerts authority over its followers or participants, a kind of mind control. In such groups, there is always a person, or a group of people, who insist that their way is the only way, that theirs is the ultimate truth.

As a spiritual teacher whose task it is to connect the world of humans with that of the gods, to forge a link between the material and spiritual worlds, The Hierophant is a *pontifex*, an ancient word that meant "maker of bridges," and that is used to designate a priest.

Therefore, when The Hierophant appears, the idea of choice is being presented. At this stage of your spiritual development, you are challenged to remain a follower or to break out and find your own individual truth. This card suggests that you have the opportunity—and often the desire—to choose your own road to salvation, to interpret the word of god in your own way. The Hierophant asks, will you continue to depend on an outside authority, or will you learn to think for yourself? The answer is yours alone, and there may be considerable conflict concerning the issue, but what you decide will affect the rest of your life.

## UPRIGHT

A traditional factor is active in your life, whether it is a religion, a philosophy, a social organization, or another authoritative group. You feel a great deal of loyalty to this tradition or group and find it supportive. You choose to live in accordance with the beliefs you share with the group or organization. You may aspire to become a leader, or you may have a close relationship with the leader. This group or tradition serves you in many ways, inspirationally, as a teacher, as emotional support. There may also be a judgmental quality involved. You are expected to follow a certain set of beliefs, and if you fail, you are called to account.

## REVERSED

You may wish to overthrow an old tradition—religious, ideological, intellectual, or cultural—that you feel is suffocating you or simply no longer serves your needs. You want to live by whatever philosophy or belief structure resonates with your true nature. You want to direct your actions your own way, even if this puts you into conflict with some established tradition. Perhaps your faith is being challenged in some way and you must re-evaluate tenets heretofore taken for granted. You want to be accountable to yourself alone.

## DESCRIPTION

One popular image on The Lovers card shows a young couple either nude or clothed, standing apart or touching. Above them is an angel-like figure with its wings spread out over them, its hands held above their heads in a gesture of blessing. The Waite deck depicts them as Adam and Eve, standing respectively before the Tree of Eternal Life and the Tree of the Knowledge of Good and Evil. Imagery in other decks suggests choice is involved as well as the possibility of union.

THE LOVERS.

Some decks include three people, as if the third party—who might be another young person or an older parental figure—were an influence in their relationship. In decks where three figures are shown, a winged, cupid-like figure on a cloud may appear and point an arrow in the direction of one of the women.

## INTERPRETATION

Although many readers interpret this card as representing romantic love, it is allegorically a statement about a union of opposites, whether those are a man and woman or inner conditions of conflict. The Lovers refers to discrimination in making choices. The male and female figures are symbols not only of human love and marriage but also of the dual nature within ourselves. We all have opposite traits and inner dichotomies that need to be reconciled. Partners of any kind often experience conflict that requires making choices and effecting reconciliation.

When The Lovers card appears, it points to the need to heal an inner rift. Although it can herald a romantic involvement, it most often turns up when a critical life decision must be made, sometimes in connection with a love relationship. There are obstacles to be overcome, both within and without. This card suggests that you are at a crossroads. You have to consider all of the ramifications of the situation and choose carefully to further your own development and to accommodate the needs of others in the situation.

In decks that show one young man and two young women on The Lovers card, the implication is that he must choose between them, another indication that this card is as much about choice as it is about partnership.

## UPRIGHT

This is a card of cooperation, of working together in coalition with others to accomplish joint purposes. It stands for attraction of any kind, not only the romantic variety, and for any venture requiring harmony, union, and cooperation. A choice between two factors of equal worth may be required, but the choice you make will be the right one. Two or more forces or people may have come together in your life in pursuit of a common goal. This may be a temporary conjunction for some specific purpose or it might be a long-term relationship.

## REVERSED

Your own disparate parts are in cooperation with each other, and warring factors of your personality are coming together. You might realize you can be beautiful and brainy at the same time, or strong and gentle simultaneously. Whatever the case, you are finding a way to bring together what was causing conflict before and melding these differences into a system of mutual support for yourself. Sometimes this card indicates a delay of some project that needs mutual cooperation or that you are trying to force cooperation among basically incompatible elements.

## DESCRIPTION

The Chariot is usually depicted as a strong male figure holding the reins of two Sphinx-like beasts, one black and one white. Sometimes the beasts are unicorns or other mythical creatures like Pegasus, the winged horse, or griffins. The charioteer is fully armored and carries a scepter suggesting royalty or that he is in the service of royalty. In some decks, he wears a belt and a skirt decorated with zodiacal glyphs, symbolic of time. On his shoulders are crescent moons indicating emotional factors and unconscious habit patterns that need to be changed.

In some decks, the charioteer holds no reins—he uses sheer willpower to keep his steeds moving together in a forward direction. The beasts pulling the chariot signify the opposing forces, which were reconciled at the stage of The Lovers and represent the person's mastery of these opposing forces and control over inner conflicts. This card suggests that before taking on outer enemies or obstacles, it is essential to be in charge of the inner opposites and stop fighting yourself. The Chariot is a symbol for the self and its direction, as is any vehicle, such as an automobile, that appears in a dream.

THE CHARIOT.

## INTERPRETATION

When The Chariot appears, there is a need to be in control of competing forces, whether these are inner conflicts, people, or a situation in your life that requires you to take command to reach your goals. Like the celebrated but seldom achieved bipartisanship of government, the solution to the problem at hand is to take the middle road between the conflicting elements.

You may feel unequal to the challenge of controlling the multiple factors of a given situation, but if you choose to just go with the flow and make the best of where it takes you, you will succeed. Once you have resolved the conflict within your own mind, even if that requires considerable struggle, you will be able to move forward. To do this, you need firm resolve—self-mastery. With a strategy determined by clear thinking and a sense of purpose, you will overcome all obstacles.

Receiving The Chariot in a reading, depending on its position in the spread, is generally favorable. It indicates you have the means to triumph over all obstacles and stay the course you have set for yourself. It can also mean that assistance is on the way as a result of your own strength and determination. It may suggest you are in the process of transforming yourself and your ways of thinking and behaving to create a firm foundation from which to go forward and achieve your desires. At this time you are keenly aware of how to use your past experience to reach a major goal and you are in touch with deep inner resources.

The wheels of the chariot signify the ever-changing life cycles. The animals are pulling in opposite directions, and the charioteer is holding the reins taut to keep the beasts in tandem—a symbolic statement of the need to master and reconcile conflicting forces, both inner and outer.

At a literal level, The Chariot relates to travel and transportation and could mean changing your mode of transport, such as buying a new car or traveling by rail or some other form of wheeled vehicle.

## UPRIGHT

Victory is assured! Things are moving fast, and transition is occurring rapidly. You are holding things together successfully, uniting opposite energies to stay on track. This is a situation where you are completely, totally involved, and happily so. Whatever task is at hand can be accomplished. Though the pace is faster than usual, you are attuned to the rhythm of it and keeping up with the changes that are happening—at your job, in a relationship, or in some community or worldly involvement. You are sensitive to the minor adjustments you must constantly make to keep things going in the right direction.

## REVERSED

When The Chariot is reversed, the changes and transitions are happening internally, but at a rapid rate. Things are moving so fast that you feel out of control and seem to be struggling to keep your head above water. It may seem that you are being pulled in two directions at once and are stressed out by the pressure. It's time to choose a direction carefully, to accept the process of inner transition as a positive one, but to do so with clarity about your direction in life. The more you can tune in to your own transition process, the more control over it you can exert.

## DESCRIPTION

The Waite and Grey decks show Strength as number Eight; many other decks, however, show Justice as Eight and Strength as Eleven. This book follows Waite's ordering of the cards.

Most decks depict Strength as a woman in relationship to a lion. Some writers see this as a struggle, but in many decks there does not appear to be any conflict. In fact, she seems to be controlling the lion and may even seem affectionate toward him. A few decks show a strong young man wrestling with the lion. The man is barehanded, which suggests that he needs no weapon.

STRENGTH.

In the Waite deck, the woman is bending over the lion in a gesture of gentleness, closing his jaws as if she expects no resistance to her touch. She is garbed in a flowing garment and wears a garland of flowers in her hair. Above her head is the symbol for infinity. In other decks, she caresses the lion, rides atop him, or stands beside him.

Although many interpreters view this card as emblematic of the struggle with one's inner animal nature, others see it as symbolic of self-confidence and inner strength, of being in harmony with one's instinctive nature. The woman is taming or making friends with the powerful force represented by the animal nature. Though the lion is clearly the more physically powerful of the two, the woman represents human courage and willpower that masters the instinctive realm not by force, but by cooperation.

## INTERPRETATION

When Strength appears in a reading, you are exhibiting moral courage and fortitude. You have learned to work in harmony with your own instinctive nature, to listen to it and hear its whisperings. As in tales of the hero's journey, the seeker often meets with animals, representative of the instinctive realm, who guide and help him on his way. Strength indicates that you have come through difficulties and learned to rely on inner strength to solve your problems.

Strength relates to the pagan goddess known as the Lady of the Beasts, who possessed understanding of the ways of nature. In ancient pagan times, this goddess reigned supreme. Later, she was personified by the Greeks as Artemis, goddess of the hunt, and by the Romans as Diana.

This is a time when faith in yourself will pay off, when your position is strong because you have made yourself strong through suffering trials and tribulations without being defeated by them. It is a time to let people around you know who you are—especially anyone who has been dominating you.

The indication is that it is the feminine principle that does the work of reconciling the mental-rational facility with that of the intuitive-instinctive nature. The feminine is always in closer touch with nature than the masculine. Whether the reading is for a man or a woman, the same meaning applies. The lesson is that we do not conquer our animal natures by brute force (which is the typical masculine mode of approach to obstacles) but by gentleness and feeling our way into rapport with the instinctive side.

Depending on the placement of the card in the spread and the question being asked, Strength indicates that what is required in the situation is for spiritual strength to replace or overcome physical strength.

## UPRIGHT

You have come through severe trials and triumphed. You have found your deep inner strength, and it will see you through whatever comes your way. You are firmly connected to the instinctual world (represented by the lion) and you are able to make friends with it and control it for your own benefit and that of others. Your positive connection to your animal self will protect and care for you. Your inner drives are in harmony with your outer needs, and your instinctive nature is supporting all that you do or hope to do. At this time, your logical mind—if it is in conflict with your intuition—is not as important in making decisions as is what you feel to be right for you. Whatever decisions you make, or actions you take, will be successful.

## REVERSED

You are struggling to gain your own in a situation that is difficult and that may be harmful to your ultimate good. As a result, you are experiencing an upsurge from your inner, instinctive nature that is calling upon you to pay attention to your own needs instead of following the orders of others. It is a time of travail, but you will eventually overcome the difficulties and come out on top. Others may think you are behaving in a way that seems to them illogical or contrary to what is normal or generally accepted. Regardless, your basic instincts of survival say this is a time for change and expressing your individuality.

# THE HERMIT

## DESCRIPTION

The Hermit is a guide figure represented as an old man, often bearded, holding a lighted lantern aloft in one hand and a staff in the other. He is usually dressed in the long robes of an anchorite or monk, plain and unadorned except for, in some decks, a knotted or tasseled cord around the waist. He radiates the wisdom of the archetypal elder figure, the sage of myth and legend.

The Hermit is generally standing, sometimes walking, looking ahead at what only he can see—your future. He is an ancient who is experienced on many levels and now functions as a teacher and guide. Mountains in the distance suggest he has reached the heights and returned to our plane to assist us in our development. He is wise in the ways of all the worlds, visible and invisible, material and immaterial.

The Hermit's slightly bent posture and serious expression link him to Father Time, or Saturn—the planet that symbolizes boundaries and limitations. His solitude suggests the periodic need to withdraw from the hectic everyday world to regain perspective through silent reflection.

## INTERPRETATION

When The Hermit appears in a reading, it can mean that a guide figure is at hand, offering help. The querent must make an effort to connect with this guide or consciously begin a search for the truth. A second interpretation is that the questioner must voluntarily withdraw from contact with the outer world for a time to search her soul for the meaning of life. The implication is that the inner work needs to be done now, and that Spirit cannot speak to you if you are distracted by the noise of everyday life. The answers lie in silence, and the work can only be done alone.

〰〰〰〰〰〰〰〰〰〰〰〰〰〰〰〰〰〰〰〰〰〰〰〰〰〰〰〰〰

The Hermit travels alone, a seeker after truth, lighting the way ahead for those who follow. He needs no trappings of rank or royalty, wears no adornment, and carries no baggage. His goal is to search and to show others their true direction. His wooden staff symbolizes his connection to the forces of nature and the instinctual realm.

〰〰〰〰〰〰〰〰〰〰〰〰〰〰〰〰〰〰〰〰〰〰〰〰〰〰〰〰〰

Whichever interpretation seems to suit the querent and the question being put to the Tarot cards, the overall meaning is the same: The time has come to reunite with the Source, whether for guidance or inner balance. Sometimes, the guide figure may represent a person, such as a counselor of some sort—a therapist or clergy person—but usually it refers to inner guidance, or getting in touch with a guide from the other side.

## UPRIGHT

The Hermit is a guide figure, waiting patiently for you to turn to him for advice. At this time, you may be involved actively in seeking guidance from the invisible world. You may be isolating yourself in some way, seeking solitude, wisdom, and inner peace. You want to gain some perspective on your life, and you are open to the inner guidance that is available to you upon request.

## REVERSED

You have been putting off giving yourself the solitude you need to sort out your life and the issues you are currently confronting. Keeping busy can be a form of denial. It is time—or long past time—for you to engage in some self-evaluation, to reflect on your aims and goals, associations, relationships, career, and life path. You may find yourself wanting to withdraw to think things through; stop avoiding it.

## DESCRIPTION

Invariably, The Wheel of Fortune card shows a wheel—often with eight spokes, a reference to the eight pagan holidays that mark the ever-turning cycles of life, death, and rebirth. The wheel is also a symbol for the sun's path across the sky. Human or mythical figures may also be attached to the wheel.

**WHEEL of FORTUNE.**

The Waite deck shows a sphinx holding a sword at the top of the wheel, calmly watching as the karmic wheel revolves. Around the wheel are letters that spell "Rota," a reference to the "Royal Road of the Tarot." The ascending figure on the right is a jackal-headed man, called Hermanubis, who is known for keen eyesight. A serpent descending on the left side represents the earth and the sexual energy that arises from it. Above and below, at the four corners of the card, are winged creatures holding open books. These correspond to the bull, the lion, the eagle, and the man, symbols of the fixed signs of the zodiac, Taurus, Leo, Scorpio, and Aquarius, respectively. In the Christian tradition, these refer to Matthew, Mark, Luke, and John.

Other decks show monkeylike figures caught on the wheel, or people in flowing robes wearing garlands in their hair, or eight young women between the spokes wearing expressions that range from joy to despair. The suggestion is that the figures are rising and falling through the various life cycles as the wheel turns. Occasionally, the wheel stands alone, obviously turning, or it is a disc decorated with symbols suspended in the sky. Sometimes a blindfolded woman is turning the wheel.

## INTERPRETATION

When The Wheel of Fortune appears in a reading, it means that something has been put in motion over which you now have little or no control. You are being forced to accept the action of the forces of destiny, to get in tune with them, and to align yourself with their aims. Generally, however, the outcome is considered favorable.

These forces already set in motion foretell of changing circumstances, usually for the better, beneficial changes that will promote your growth and advancement. Balance may be an issue if you are resisting change, but you now have no choice but to go along with whatever process is working in your life. The Wheel of Fortune is a reminder that every period of intense activity must be followed by a fallow time of rest and inactivity. Where you are in your own personal cycle will be shown by the other cards in the spread. This card almost always heralds good fortune coming as a result of what you yourself have put into motion, even if you aren't totally aware of what you have done to initiate the process. You may have applied for a new job, met a new person, begun a romance, decided to take a college course, or had a chance encounter that got the ball rolling—or the wheel turning. It means a new phase, possibly the need to make an important decision, or even a totally unexpected circumstance developing that will change your life.

The Wheel of Fortune is linked to the three Fates. One spins the thread of life, the second weaves it, and the third cuts it. Thus, The Wheel of Fortune is a reminder of the mysterious cycles of life, death, and rebirth and of the invisible forces that measure them out to each of us.

## UPRIGHT

You have done something—quit a job, made travel reservations, begun or ended a relationship, or opted out of a friendship or other situation. Destiny has been set in motion, and all will turn out as it is intended. There's very little more you have to do except to go with the flow. There may be unexpected turns of events—such as meeting people while you are on a journey or receiving an offer of some sort—but they too are part of the grand plan for your life. This card is the precursor of good fortune.

## REVERSED

You are holding back your own destiny by your refusal to make the necessary changes or take the required actions. Refusing to set things in motion is causing stagnation and frustration. Although you rationalize the fact that you are standing still, you are uncomfortable with the situation. You think you are waiting for the propitious time, but fear of the unknown is blocking you. You may be fantasizing about what you want to do, but you have to take action before anything can happen. You may experience delays in your projects because of lack of commitment. Ask the universe to show you the way and fearlessly follow the direction you are given. It's time to quit being wishy-washy and get on with what you already know you need to do.

## DESCRIPTION

The Justice card usually depicts a female figure, robed, sometimes armored, and crowned. She holds an upright sword in one hand and in the other perfectly balanced scales. In some modern decks, she is either a nude figure with arms outstretched in absolute even balance, or she is shown standing between a large set of scales while holding a smaller set.

JUSTICE.

Unlike the contemporary image of Justice as blindfolded, this Justice is open-eyed, suggesting that divine justice rather than the laws of man are at work here. She stares straight ahead, suggesting that divine justice is not bound by human limitations and that divine law is not subject to error and bias.

## INTERPRETATION

When the Justice card appears in a reading, it can indicate that an actual legal matter is pending or being considered. Whatever the situation, you must weigh many factors to make a reasoned and factual assessment, i.e., judgment, of the matter at hand. The Justice card warns you to receive guidance from your inner self, not to rely solely on human advisors. Also, it cautions prudence and care, the need to deliberate calmly and carefully before taking action or concluding an outcome.

If other people are involved, you would be wise to take their point of view into consideration, for issues of fairness are paramount now. You can expect legal matters, if a part of the circumstances, to proceed smoothly, fairly, and in a dispassionate manner. Be confident that Justice will prevail as a result of your own temperate behavior and rational thought. Depending on what other cards appear in the spread, a third party could come to your aid and help you get the fair outcome you deserve. This card can also represent anyone involved with the legal profession—a lawyer, a judge, witnesses, law enforcement officers, and the like.

---

Justice may describe a matter in which some sort of rectification is necessary, where wrongs must be righted, in a spiritual or personal sense, regardless of whether any laws have been broken. This is a card of karma and suggests you are reaping what you have sown.

---

## UPRIGHT

You are concerned with external circumstances, waiting for the right time to act. You may be seeking justice in personal or business affairs, or you may be involved with a lawsuit. In any case, it is important to resolve the situation in a way that is fair to all participants. You must create a balance, not only of power but also in terms of your emotional reactions to the situation at hand. This is a time for moderation in all things, for creating harmony to facilitate relationships. Your judgment is good at this time, and you are not swayed by personal considerations or bias.

## REVERSED

Justice in reverse indicates delays in legal matters or unfairness in some other situation, and you might become angry and hostile. If you are the person in power, you may be unduly severe in meting out punishment. If you are in the powerless position, you may be festering with resentment over being treated unfairly. Your state of equilibrium is out of whack, and you may be swinging from one extreme to another. The antidote is to balance your own life and become less dependent upon outside influences.

# THE HANGED MAN

## DESCRIPTION

The Hanged Man is a tantalizing figure. Usually a male, hanging upside down by one leg, The Hanged Man's expression is serene, as if he is thoroughly enjoying his state. Suspended as he is by one foot, he appears to be engaged in a rather bizarre form of meditation or ritual.

In the Waite deck, The Hanged Man is shown hanging from a tree. Its roots are in the ground and the crosspiece that supports him sprouts leaves. Some authorities say this is the Tree of Life itself. Around The Hanged Man's head is a golden halo, like the rays of the sun. Yellow is the color of Mercury, the planet of the mind. Other decks picture only the horizontal beam, but it too has leaves on it, showing that it is living wood.

THE HANGED MAN.

## INTERPRETATION

Many writers see The Hanged Man as a card of self-sacrifice and martyrdom, but others view this card as voluntary surrender to the process of achieving enlightenment. It may require giving up superficial pleasures and trivial activities in pursuit of a more spiritual way of life. The word "sacrifice" derives from the Latin *sacra fice*, which means "to make sacred." Therefore, The Hanged Man may represent a sacred pursuit.

When this card appears in a reading, depending on its position in the layout, the person has usually received a call to follow a less materialistic way of life. You are ready for whatever personal sacrifice is needed, or you are preparing to make such a gesture. You may need to pause momentarily and suspend ordinary activities to better realize where you are headed spiritually.

This card can indicate that a new commitment to the development of the inner self is demanded. You might need to spend time alone to re-evaluate just what is and what is not important to you. It may be very difficult to let go of old patterns, but letting go is essential to your continued growth.

><><><><><><><><><><><><><><><><><><><><><><><><><><><><><><><><><><><><><><><><><

Often, The Hanged Man signifies going through a major transformation, perhaps caused by illness or some loss. The result has shaken up your old way of life and made you realize that there is more to life than money, material goods, and physical reality.

><><><><><><><><><><><><><><><><><><><><><><><><><><><><><><><><><><><><><><><><><

## UPRIGHT

You are suspended between the past and the future; a new direction for your life is in the making. It is a time for a new perspective. Look at things from a different angle to make necessary readjustments. You need to make a clean break with the past and concentrate on becoming spiritually attuned. Readjustment is needed, but the good news is there's no hurry. Take your time and make the right decisions about where you truly want to take your life at this time and for the long term. Pay attention to your inner development and be prepared to dance to a different drummer in the future.

## REVERSED

You are at a crossroads but are at a standstill because you have become stuck on the material plane and are neglecting your spiritual development. You may be in denial about your real needs, which could be causing depression, dissatisfaction, or apathy. You feel that any effort will be futile. This is because you are not being true to your inner self. You may be sacrificing some part of your life unnecessarily because of a martyr complex and a refusal to make decisions. It's time to end such behavior and commit yourself to a worthwhile goal that will lead to your higher good. This may require turning your world upside down.

## DESCRIPTION

The Death card tends to frighten people who see it come up in a reading, but despite its grim depiction it symbolizes the transforming powers of life, death, and rebirth. Many decks picture a skeleton with a scythe grinning toothily and wearing a black, hooded robe. The Waite deck pictures Death as a man in black armor riding a white charger, suggesting the perpetual movement of the cycles of life and death.

DEATH.

The knight carries a banner on which is embroidered the mystical white rose, symbol of pure and true love. The rose with five petals represents the five senses of material life combined with the immortality of the heart, or soul. Greeting the knight with hands outstretched in blessing or supplication is a priest figure wearing a mitered cardinal's hat. Two children look on in awe. In the background, the sun is rising, a sign of resurrection, over a body of water representing the unconscious realm.

Other decks show barren backgrounds; sometimes severed body parts are lying about randomly. One deck features the four horses of the Apocalypse riding through a stormy sky. Another presents a hooded, faceless figure standing in a woods, who appears to be supporting with one arm a huge white rose that dominates the card.

## INTERPRETATION

The Death card in a reading rarely foreshadows a physical death. What it means is the end, or death, of a cycle. Whenever a stage in one's life ends, there is a need for mourning. It is only the refusal to accept that something is ending—trying desperately to hold on to what is clearly over—that causes trouble. Employing cosmetic means to stave off the approach of age, for instance, is a useless effort to avoid the inevitable. What gives importance and meaning to this card is the querent's acceptance of the change that cannot be avoided. Thus, in essence, the ultimate message of the Death card is the promise that new life follows disintegration.

## UPRIGHT

Contrary to the grim illustration, the Death card is actually positive, for it indicates a transformation for the better. It does not portend actual physical death. Usually, the person is experiencing a metamorphosis of some sort, a destruction of the old, outworn circumstances that have been holding back new development. Patterns you once found workable are no longer effective. The old ways must be destroyed to make room for the new that is coming into being.

## REVERSED

You are putting off making necessary changes, usually out of fear. You feel that others are standing in your way, but it's really yourself who's blocking you. You're stuck in old habit patterns that you know need to be changed, but you don't want to put forth the effort to alter them even though you are unhappy with the current situation. Whether you recognize it or not, you are going through some internal changes that will eventually lead to external reforms. But at the moment you would rather not participate. You may be depressed or in a state of apathy, the result of refusing to accept the necessary process of psychological death, which leads to rebirth. The way out is to face up to your stagnation, frustration, and unhappiness. Jettison any relationships that aren't working. Begin to make the decisions that will throw out the old and ring in the new.

## DESCRIPTION

This lovely card often features a winged angel—male, female, or androgynous. In the Waite deck, the angel is standing in a stream bordered by flowers, with the rising sun shining in the background. In most decks, the figure is pouring liquid—the elixir of life—from a golden vessel into a silver one in a continuous stream, suggesting the interplay of the material and spiritual worlds and the eternal flow of the waters of life. The word "vessel" is related to the Great Mother goddesses of antiquity, and the body is often referred to as the vessel of the soul. Thus, both the angelic figure and the cups are symbolic references to the feminine principles of cooperation, balance, harmony, receptivity, and creativity.

TEMPERANCE.

## INTERPRETATION

Temperance, as its name suggests, is about moderation in all things. When Temperance appears in a reading, depending on its position in the spread, you are being cautioned to have patience, which may be difficult under the circumstances. However, the circumstances of your situation will teach you to wait calmly when it seems like nothing is happening.

The person who receives Temperance in a reading is not in a position to hurry matters along. The only course is to sit and wait for things to move in their own time. The trick is to make the waiting constructive. This is one of the great lessons of the Zen masters. Learning to do nothing mindfully is a milestone on the spiritual path. It's of vital importance to know that there are times when nothing can be done and nothing needs to be done. Therein lies the state of grace.

~~~~~~~~~~~~~~~~~~~~~~~~~~~~~~~~~~~~~~~~~~~~~~~~~~~~~~~~~~~~~~~~~~~~

The word "temperance" is derived from the Latin *temperare*, which means to "moderate, blend, or mix together harmoniously." Interestingly, this card was earlier named Time, which is a key to its underlying meaning.

~~~~~~~~~~~~~~~~~~~~~~~~~~~~~~~~~~~~~~~~~~~~~~~~~~~~~~~~~~~~~~~~~~~~

## UPRIGHT

You are being asked to blend things in a harmonious way, and you have the ability to achieve this goal. You are learning to temper your ego needs with the legitimate needs of the spirit within. This is a time of inner growth and outer harmony. With patience, you can blend disparate elements—whether they are raw materials, resources, personnel, or ideas—into a harmonious whole.

## REVERSED

Things seem to be stalled. There's not much you can do at the present except to let things work themselves out, which they will in time. Patience is the key, for trying to force inharmonious elements together will only cause bad feelings and poor results, like mixing oil and water. This is a time to concentrate on blending the different parts of yourself together into a new form—of combining your psychological, emotional, and spiritual elements into a new you. Temper whatever inner conditions you have that make you feel out of balance.

## DESCRIPTION

Many decks picture a medieval Christian-type devil, complete with horns, hooves, a hairy tail, and a pitchfork. Usually at the devil's feet are two small, human-like figures, one male and one female, with chains around their necks that are attached to the block upon which The Devil sits. However, it is important to note that the chains are loose and the people could easily slip them off, suggesting self-imposed limitations.

**THE DEVIL.**

Whatever form The Devil takes in various decks, he is usually pretty scary-looking. Occasionally, he is bat-like or stylized depending on the theme of the deck and its designer's inclinations toward the figure. The Gilded Tarot portrays him as a muscular young man, whose face is half-hidden beneath a helmet-mask. In some decks, he has an inverted pentagram over his head or on his brow. In one deck, there is no devil at all, only two nude figures chained to a symbolically decorated block, straining toward an open doorway at the end of a long tunnel.

The variety of illustrations implies widely differing opinions of the card's meaning. For some, the devil is a creature of consummate evil; for others the devil is a mythical creature. Many psychologically oriented people see the devil as a symbol of human indulgence, ignorance, egotism, greed, and irresponsibility. Thus, the illustration appearing on the card represents a point of view as well as the traditional meanings associated with the card.

# INTERPRETATION

Superficially, The Devil appears to be one of the more alarming cards of the Major Arcana. However, he does not represent satanic forces with evil intent, and it is important to remember this when doing readings. He is the horned god of pagan times, connected to the fertility rites banned by the Catholic Church, which feared the power of pagan rituals, especially those including sexual activity.

When The Devil shows up in a reading, depending upon his position in the spread, he is telling you that you need to re-evaluate your relationship to material things, which are keeping you chained. It's time to look at whatever is limiting you and holding you back from personal growth, especially abusive, obsessive, or harmful relationships. You are being called upon to confront your fears about financial security and social and material success—the things of this world. The Devil is a reality check.

You need to recognize and acknowledge things you don't like about yourself—your personality, body, or temperament. It's time to let go of old fears, hang-ups, inhibitions, and ways you manipulate others to satisfy your needs instead of taking responsibility for yourself in a positive manner. Often there is a sexual component involved that is having a harmful effect on your whole life. Or there could be a nonsexual relationship that binds you and that must end before you can grow further.

◇◇◇◇◇◇◇◇◇◇◇◇◇◇◇◇◇◇◇◇◇◇◇◇◇◇◇◇◇◇◇◇◇◇◇◇◇◇◇◇◇◇◇◇◇◇◇◇◇◇◇◇◇◇◇◇◇◇◇◇◇◇◇◇◇◇

The devil is related to the old pagan god Great Pan, a god of nature and the natural processes of the physical world, including sex. The Greek form of Pan was Dionysus, who was known for cavorting with satyrs and in whose honor wild and uninhibited rituals that included a sexual free-for-all were held annually.

◇◇◇◇◇◇◇◇◇◇◇◇◇◇◇◇◇◇◇◇◇◇◇◇◇◇◇◇◇◇◇◇◇◇◇◇◇◇◇◇◇◇◇◇◇◇◇◇◇◇◇◇◇◇◇◇◇◇◇◇◇◇◇◇◇◇

Whatever the situation, you are the only one who can change it. The two chained figures on the card represent bondage to the material realm. Their loose chains indicate your potential for attaining freedom by relinquishing obsessive ambition and excessive attachment to the things of this world.

## UPRIGHT

The Devil is a mythical creature with no real substance, but symbolically it represents the bondage that we create and maintain for ourselves. There may be obstacles in the environment that you find frustrating, or you may feel your options are narrowing. Someone else may be involved, but you have the ability to free yourself from the situation by using your willpower.

## REVERSED

You feel trapped in a situation over which you feel you have no control, but close examination will reveal that your own attitudes and beliefs are causing the problem. The solution is to carefully examine your beliefs to learn how they are restricting you. Be careful of any quick fix to your problems, which are structural and not superficial. If you are willing to do the hard work, both on the inner and outer planes, you can solve the issues and achieve success on your own. Remember that Saturn rules The Devil card, and Saturn's influences are long-term.

## DESCRIPTION

The Tower usually depicts a stone tower of fortress-like construction, such as those still remaining from medieval times in Europe. The Tower is in the process of falling down or being destroyed, most often by fire or lightning.

In the Waite deck, and some others, The Tower's crown is being blown off by the fiery impact. The blast catapults human figures out of the windows. The implication is that the forces of heaven are angry and attacking the structure, causing flaming debris to fly out in all directions.

THE TOWER.

## INTERPRETATION

Like the Death card and The Devil, The Tower tends to strike alarm and fear into anyone in whose reading it appears, and indeed many writers assign a fully negative meaning to this card. The Tower does not necessarily represent ruin and devastation, although its appearance usually does herald swift and dramatic change—sometimes shocking and extremely upsetting change.

It is important to keep in mind that the querent has usually brought the situation on herself by ignoring or denying that something is rotten and needs restructuring or deconstructing. Most likely, the querent is already well aware of a pressing need to make changes, but she is steadfastly refusing to take action. Then along comes a circumstance, such as losing a job or getting a divorce, having an accident or a financial setback, that forces the person to face reality.

There's no question this card signifies the crumbling of an old and outworn structure. It demands that you begin to deal seriously with your life collapsing all around you instead of, like the Roman emperor

Nero, fiddling while your house burns. Any number of possibilities exist—breaking off an unsatisfactory or destructive relationship, quitting a stifling job, casting off false materialistic values, confronting long-buried issues of guilt and shame, shucking the social conventions that limit your progress, selling your over-mortgaged house and living more simply, or ridding yourself of burdensome possessions. The list is endless, but the querent nearly always knows what the issue is and that she is imprisoned by a self-created fortress, whether for protection, safety, or from fear of facing the unknown.

The Tower parallels the Old Testament story of the Tower of Babel, which was a massive structure intended to reach all the way up to god in his heaven. It is also known as "La Maison Dieu" (The House of God) and the Falling Tower, or the Tower of Destruction.

The message of The Tower is that you must destroy the old structures before they destroy you, so you can become free. Otherwise, they may be shattered by seemingly outside influences (which you have actually created yourself). In the wake of the chaos, a new order will grow. What was unsound will come tumbling down. You can pick and choose among the rubble to decide what is worth saving, and from that, rebuild your life in accordance with who you truly are.

## UPRIGHT

Many people interpret The Tower as representing catastrophe, but whatever disruption or adversity it heralds is for the best. The Tower represents the overthrow of false ideas and old habit patterns that need to be gotten rid of. In this sense, it is not a negative card but a positive one. Sometimes, there is indeed some kind of loss—personal or financial. But careful examination of all of the factors will generally show that the catastrophic event could have been foreseen if you had only been aware and willing to face facts. The Tower is related to Uranus, the planet of unexpected, lightning-fast events. What is destroyed in conjunction with this card has served its purpose and needs to go.

## REVERSED
You are refusing to change old habit patterns, and you will suffer continued disruption in the form of unforeseen difficulties until you finally get the message that it's time to make some changes in your life. You may be confused about just who and what you are. At a deep level, you are being prepared for the changes that must eventually take place, but you are resisting what your inner self knows already. It is possible for you to alter fixed beliefs and limited ideas about your identity. Once you do, there will be far-reaching ramifications and a new sense of freedom in your life.

## DESCRIPTION

This lovely card usually portrays a nude female figure in or beside a pool of water, pouring from two jugs, one held in each hand. In the Waite deck, she kneels and pours the contents of one pitcher into the stream and the contents of the other into the ground, showing the connection between the two feminine elements: earth and water.

THE STAR.

The background of this card always displays stars; often, one directly above the figure's head is much larger than the others. Many decks show seven subsidiary stars, sometimes arranged to reflect the portal or two-pillar theme, sometimes set in a circle or a halo-like form around her. The stars sparkle above a pastoral setting—trees, mountains, birds, flowers. If trees appear in the image, they may be configured on either side of her, another echo of the portal or pillars. The colors are usually bright, often with yellow (the color of optimism) predominating, although some decks depict a nighttime scene.

The naked woman represents unveiled truth and purity. The jugs she holds contain the waters of life. Some of the water is being returned to the Source, some is being used to infuse the land with new life.

## INTERPRETATION

The Star is a universal symbol of hope. Its appearance can signal the end of the travails represented by some of the earlier cards, symbolizing that a new and happier phase of life is coming into being. We see shooting stars as harbingers of good luck. From earliest times humans have been awed and fascinated by the star-spangled sky and the constellations.

The Star in a reading is like looking up at the bright starry sky on a clear night and seeing all the magnificence of the universe. It stimulates us to ponder the great potential of each and every human being for growth, inspiration, intuition, inner wisdom, and happiness.

Although The Star does not usually point to any specific planetary transit, as do some of the other Major Arcana cards, it does have a strong connection to astrology in general, for the zodiac signs relate to constellations. When The Star appears in a reading, it is a good time to have your horoscope read or to begin studying astrology yourself. A gate has opened for you to new possibilities. This card portends good fortune, creative inspiration, spiritual growth, help from unseen forces, and wishes come true. It marks a time of fulfillment.

## UPRIGHT

At this time you are experiencing a new flow of energy and self-confidence. You feel good about yourself and your place in the universe. You have arrived at a significant place, for which you have been preparing yourself. You are receiving assistance both from the invisible world and from the material world. Good things are in the offing—money, possessions, love, recognition, or assistance—because you are freely flowing with the pure energy of the universe. Full of faith and trust in life and its many processes, you are setting new goals for the future and opening the door to new opportunities in your career or relationships.

## REVERSED

When The Star is reversed, it says that you are seeking your own path in a private way, without regard for the outside world and its benefits. You may be feeling alone, withdrawn, even resentful of outer obligations at this time, because your inner need is great. You may recently have experienced some disappointment, and this might have brought on a mood of pessimism that has caused you to turn inward for comfort. This is a necessary step. You need "repair time," including silence and solitude, to attune yourself with your inner needs. When you do, you will begin to re-energize yourself in concert with who you truly are.

# THE MOON

## DESCRIPTION

The Moon is a magical, mysterious card emblematic of the unconscious and the invisible realm of dreams, imagination, and psychic impressions. Usually the moon occupies the top half of the card, sometimes shown in both its full and crescent phases with the crescent enclosed in the full circle. In the Waite deck, drops of water fall from the moon, raining down on two canines, a dog and a wolf, who bay at the moon. Two towers, one on either side, reflect the portal theme. At the bottom of the card is a pool or pond of water from which crawls a crab (symbol of the astrological sign Cancer, which is ruled by the moon),

THE MOON.

crawfish, or lobster. The water suggests the moon's link with the tides, the earth, the emotions, and the unconscious realm.

Some authorities say the animals represent our opposite tendencies—the wolf, the untamed inner animal nature; the dog, the domesticated, daily persona we show to the world. But canines and the moon have deep mythological roots that relate to the underworld. In addition, the dog indicates psychic ability as it is able to follow an invisible trail and locate what cannot be seen.

## INTERPRETATION

Astrologically, the moon represents the soul, which is the link between spirit (sun) and matter (earth). The moon is feminine: It symbolizes what we feel and how we respond. Therefore, it is emblematic of all that is receptive in human nature: the subconscious, the emotions, the instincts, and the automatic functions of the body. The lunar self is the channel for the flow of the universal, or divine, source, and as such, the moon has great power. It affects everything and everyone on earth, from the ocean's tides to the moods and reproductive cycles of humans.

Therefore, when The Moon appears in a reading, it suggests that you should be paying more attention to your inner self, your lunar self. It advises you to illuminate your deepest nature. In its diffuse light, we can often see more clearly than in the glare of the noonday sun. The light of the sun enables us to see the world around us, but the moon allows us to illuminate what springs naturally from inside ourselves.

The Moon card can point to a need to nurture yourself or to care for your health. For artistic people, its presence in a reading may mark a time of increased imagination and creativity.

During the hours of night, our subtle senses are more open and receptive to our inner spiritual harmony. When The Moon appears in a reading, it is time to attend to your dreams, feelings, instincts, and intuition.

Although traditionally The Moon card can indicate deceit and self-deception, confinement and undoing, these conditions are usually a result of ignoring your own inner promptings. If you get "taken"—especially emotionally—it's because you were letting your rational mind override your feelings. The Moon card's appearance also notifies you to take care of loose ends connected to the past, especially to your mother or other females.

The Moon is the symbol for the goddess, whose three aspects represent the three faces of the Great Triple goddess. As the newborn crescent, the moon is the maiden, the virgin—not chaste, but belonging to herself alone, not bound to any man. At the full moon, she is the mature woman, sexual and maternal, giver of life. At the end of her cycle, the waning moon about to turn dark represents the crone whose years have ripened into wisdom.

## UPRIGHT

The Moon says that you are aware of the need to tune in to your lunar energies. You are now perceiving the reality of your inner nature more clearly, becoming more aware of the shadings and nuances of feelings and inner perceptions. The Moon also suggests psychic ability. You can tune in to other people's vibrations because you are connected to the information network of the invisible world. Pay attention to hunches and dreams. This is also a good time to develop your psychic skills.

## REVERSED

Your soul is calling for help, trying to get your attention. You may have been ignoring your lunar needs—self-nurturance, artistic expression, and receptivity. The demands of the day—the masculine side—are overwhelming you, and you need time out to reconnect with the feminine side of life. You have allowed the pressures of the outside world to throw you out of balance, and you feel disconnected from your true self. It's time to rest and reflect.

The moon's energies change continually, segueing from one phase into the next. After the night of the dark moon, for example, the energy of the new moon begins increasing, and two weeks later culminates in the full moon. The energy of the full moon can usually be felt two days before total fullness is achieved and continues for another day or two afterward, diminishing as the waning phase takes over.

To increase your sensitivity to the moon and your lunar self, sit facing the direction of the visible moon. If possible, position yourself in front of a window or go outside where the rays of the moon can shine on you. If you cannot see her, acknowledge her by closing your eyes and imagining the beautiful silver crescent or disk in the dark sky. Sit quietly for several minutes until you can feel the moon's energy contacting you. Imagine her vibrations entering your body, connecting your soul to her. Feel the magnetic pull of the moon on your sensitivities, just as they pull the tides, and allow yourself to be touched within by her softly glowing light. Let the moon illuminate your dark night of the soul, inspiring and uplifting you.

# THE SUN

## DESCRIPTION

The Sun card features a blazing sun, sometimes with a face, with sunbeams radiating out from it. Beneath the sun, in the Waite deck, a smiling nude child is riding a white horse. Behind him, a banner unfurls, held up by a winged staff. In the background, huge sunflowers grow against a stone wall.

Some decks show two children with their arms around each other; other decks picture a young couple holding hands. The child, or children, are clearly very happy. The Sun is the planetary ruler of Leo, which is linked with children, pleasure, and creativity. The astrological sun also

THE SUN.

rules the heart, the center of the body and the personality. The Sun card represents life itself, for the sun gives life to everything on earth. The Sun suggests vitality, confidence, achievement, ego-attainment, and success in all endeavors. It is emblematic of the proverb, "May the Sun shine on all you do," the implication being that sunshine brings joy.

## INTERPRETATION

When The Sun card appears, it is an indication that your past work is now bearing fruit, a concept that is symbolized by the child or children. Along with The Moon, it implies the union between the unconscious realm of creativity (moon) and the conscious realm of manifestation (sun). Whether the birth represented is a biological child or a creative project, the outcome is a happy one. It is a time when good things come into your life—success, optimism, achievement, health, general good fortune, and happiness.

When The Sun turns up, it brightens any negative cards in the spread—no matter where The Sun appears in the spread. His influence is always beneficial, suggesting prosperity, enthusiasm, honors, public recognition, and attainment. You are happy to be alive because you feel it is the dawning of a new day. Any special efforts or ventures, such as taking a test or making a presentation, will turn out favorably.

In the wake of the demise of the Great Mother goddess as the sole divinity, the Sun, which represents the masculine principle, came to be worshipped as the central deity in many cultures. The ancient Egyptians, after eons of a pantheon of goddesses and gods, under the leadership of the pharaoh Akhenaton, were persuaded, albeit reluctantly, to accept a single god—known as Ra, Amun-Ra, or Aton (all of which were names for the Sun)—which Akhenaton believed was the god of all gods. The Greeks called their sun god Helios, whom the Romans named Apollo.

## UPRIGHT

Generally considered a positive card, The Sun relates to energy, vitality, confidence, success, and good times. It signifies a time of new beginnings, of things going well, of accomplishment, success, and contentment. You feel cheerful and self-confident, full of life and vitality, ready to undertake new projects and make changes for the better. Whatever you are planning, you feel a great deal of enthusiasm for it and aren't worried about the outcome. You may be starting more than one project, or upgrading something in your life, such as moving to a better-paying, more satisfying job, remodeling your home, or moving to a sunnier climate.

The appearance of The Sun in a reading can foreshadow a reward for your previous striving and suffering with a day at the beach. The Sun card can indicate you are going to take a wonderful vacation in the sun where you can relax and let go of your worries.

# REVERSED

All of the previously mentioned qualities apply to the reversed Sun, because it is never a negative card. However, the reversed position indicates that there will be delays or that you will have to make some adjustments you hadn't planned on. Maybe you need to spruce up your appearance for that new job—get a new haircut or a new wardrobe to show yourself at your very best. Now is the time to explore new and more effective ways to express who you are to the outside world.

## DESCRIPTION

The Judgment card visually seems rather negative. In the Waite deck, a winged figure, who some call the angel Gabriel, emerges from a cloud and blows a trumpet. Beneath him are several nude figures of men and women looking up, hearing the trumpet's blast. Their arms are outstretched, and they seem to have risen from coffins or the earth itself. Their expressions reveal awe tinged with fear.

JUDGEMENT.

Of all the allegorical symbolism of the Major Arcana, this is the most purely Christian, suggesting the feared Day of Judgment, when god will judge all souls and apportion out rewards or punishments accordingly. However, this is not a totally Christian idea; the Egyptians and other cultures also expressed the notion of the soul being judged. The goddess Maat, for instance, weighs the soul against her Feather of Truth.

Whether seen from a Christian point of view (which these medieval images represent) or from a universal one, the idea behind the symbols is that of an awakening.

## INTERPRETATION

When the Judgment card appears, what is being awakened is a sense of a higher self within. Sometimes the card coincides with a person turning away from a traditional set of beliefs toward one that better suits his personal philosophy of life. Judgment represents the end of something—an old way of life, a cycle that is finished. It is a time to seek new direction, to make adjustments that reflect who you truly are—perhaps by breaking away from your conventional way of life and believing.

Generally speaking, this is a positive card symbolizing regeneration and rebirth into wholeness after a period of confusion and a sense of confinement (shown by the coffins). You may have been feeling "dead" in your old life. When Judgment appears, you have the unique opportunity to relive, to enliven yourself and your environment by making the appropriate changes. What is ending is doubt and indecision, depression and despair, fear and inhibition. It's a time of new freedom to be yourself.

## UPRIGHT

You've had a wake-up call from the universe and are now ready to step into a new phase of your maturing process. Your life is fairly settled now, and you are letting things grow and mature at a steady pace, not trying to hurry the process. A new phase in your life is coming into being as the natural result of your maturity—like a tree that has gone through the flowering stage bears fruit as the product of its maturity. You may get important news that will prove beneficial, or you may acquire new knowledge that will bring you joy and a sense of fulfillment. Health improves, and problems are easily solved.

## REVERSED

Interior biological and psychological factors are at work, and you have little or no control over them. You may be thinking about making some changes, which are being signaled by these inner timing mechanisms. This process may be throwing you into a state of confusion as you aren't sure just how to handle what's happening. Nonetheless, you are facing a new phase in your life and must make your peace with it. Emotionally, you may be called upon to grow up. Judgment reversed can also indicate frustrating delays or postponements, a materialistic view of life, refusal to take charge, possible loss or separation, and the need to cope with these life changes.

# THE WORLD

## DESCRIPTION

In many decks, The World card shows a young woman, sometimes nude or wearing a long scarf. The scarf covers her genitals but leaves her breasts bare. In each hand, she holds a double-ended wand that points both upward and downward, suggesting, "As above, so below." In the Waite deck, she is surrounded by an oval-shaped wreath.

THE WORLD.

As with The Wheel of Fortune card, to which The World is related, the four corners of the card feature a bull, a lion, an eagle, and a man—representing the four fixed signs of the zodiac: Taurus, Leo, Scorpio, and Aquarius. These elemental figures also depict the four directions. In the Waite deck, the wreath is bound at the top and bottom by ribbons in the shape of the infinity symbol that is found on both The Magician and Strength cards.

## INTERPRETATION

This is the last numbered card of the Major Arcana. It represents balance and support by unseen forces and symbolizes the end of the spiritual journey begun by The Fool. To embark upon the spiritual journey is to invite unseen forces to interact with us. These creative energies manifest in many ways, and often serve as guides. Guides bring us into grace and show the way. To encounter a guide—and they come in many guises—is to enter another realm, a place of great powers and, sometimes, great secrets. This realm belongs to the invisible world, although its denizens can, like angels, assume human or animal form. To interface with this world is to be impacted in a way that is life-changing. With guides, we enter a world of supreme power—not the power of the material world but of the invisible order that supports and nourishes our world and our lives here. It is the realm of the sacred.

When The World card appears in a reading, it is a signal that you have been guided to the successful conclusion of your spiritual journey. At this, the final stage, you will receive what is rightfully yours because you have earned it. Now you are and feel whole, complete. You are refreshed from your long journey and ready to begin anew at a higher level.

## UPRIGHT

Success in all endeavors is assured. Everything is available to you—success, happiness, harmony. All is right with the world. Whatever you do now will prosper—a career change, a move to another place, a new relationship, recognition, rewards, acclaim. This is the end of an old cycle and the beginning of a new one. You have mastered the complexities of your own inner nature and feel supported by your inner resources. This is a time of supreme self-confidence and victory. You have put your trust where it belongs—in a Higher Power—and you will reap the rewards. At this time, many possibilities and opportunities are available to you, and you are completely free to choose what pleases you.

## REVERSED

You are being presented with a multiplicity of choices and aren't sure which one to make. You may be experiencing new facets of your own self or investigating different levels of reality. Or you may be rejecting new ideas being offered out of fear or a limited understanding. Now is the time to face the fact that the universe is a more complex place than you have been willing to admit.

# THE SUIT OF WANDS

In medieval Tarot decks, the suit of Wands represented the working class—those individuals who were attached to the noble houses as serfs. They had little choice but to follow the trade of their fathers, and they were usually apprenticed out at an early age to learn some difficult and unpleasant task. Today the Wands have come to represent whatever work you do and how you express your talents, as well as your ability to overcome odds and achieve success.

# INTERPRETING THE WANDS

In a larger sense, the Wands are linked with creativity, drive, energy, enthusiasm, willpower, and outer-world activities. They describe attitudes, abilities, and situations that offer the potential for success, perhaps through utilizing your talents and imagination, even though you may have to overcome obstacles in the process. Artists and craftspeople, for instance, may find that Wands appear in their readings frequently. Financial achievement may or may not be a factor; self-expression and fulfilling your potential are more important.

How the Wands are pictured varies considerably from deck to deck. Generally speaking, Wands are positive cards. The colors tend to be bright (yellow stands for optimism, red for action) and the designs or scenarios depicted are usually cheerful. Wands may be symbolized as branches sprouting leaves or flowers, wooden staffs, crude clubs, poles, scepter-like rods, or flaming torches. Sometimes these images are mixed within the same deck. As representative of the Fire element and masculine force, Wands are obvious phallic symbols.

The King of Wands is usually shown as a dignified man, seated on a throne, robed and crowned. A positive and powerful figure, he is clearly in command of the situation, confident and at ease. He holds a full-length staff or rod, generally upright but sometimes leaning against his shoulder. In some decks, this King faces sideways, and whether he is looking toward or away from other cards in a spread will have a bearing on his relationship to the reading.

KING of WANDS.

## UPRIGHT

Upright, the King represents a man of status and wealth, an influential and independent person who is inclined to help those he cares about. You can rely on his honesty, intelligence, loyalty, and fair-mindedness, and you are sure to get good advice from him. If the King does not represent an actual person in your life, he can refer to a situation, which is exactly as it appears to be with no hint of deception. This card can indicate that good fortune is coming your way, perhaps in the form of good news, a promotion, or an inheritance.

## REVERSED

The King of Wands reversed indicates delays in a business or creative project you are starting; however, nothing really problematic is standing in your way. If the King represents a person to you, the man he stands for will be available but won't go out of his way to help you. He won't block your efforts. He may even approve of what you are trying to accomplish on your own and lend moral support. But don't expect overt or tangible assistance.

# QUEEN OF WANDS

The Queen of Wands is pictured as a statuesque woman of regal bearing. She holds a tall staff in one hand, a symbol of her authority. Often she sits on a throne, robed and crowned, but some decks show her as a well-dressed matron figure.

QUEEN of WANDS.

## UPRIGHT

Socially prominent, this Queen represents a woman who is in a position of authority and shines in her endeavors. She is a "lioness"—warm, generous, and loving. She is honorable, creative, intelligent, friendly, and mature. Her advice is well worth taking, and she will be a loyal confidante or provide valuable assistance. A natural leader, she may be the head of a business, social, or philanthropic organization, or a political figure. If this Queen does not represent an actual person, she indicates that now is a good time for you to move forward in any business or creative venture you are planning. If the Queen represents you, she is an indication that you have the qualities within yourself that you need to succeed.

## REVERSED

If the Queen of Wands is reversed, she can represent a powerful woman who demands control over your affairs in return for her advice, support, and/or financial assistance. She wants to control social situations for her own advantage. If the Queen does not represent an actual person, the reversed card can be a warning to be careful in any business deals with women. She also advises you to avoid giving offense to the socially powerful, and to be aware of deception, greed, and jealousy.

# KNIGHT OF WANDS

The Knight of Wands is usually depicted as a young man on a rearing horse, in a mode of forward action. He is brandishing the wand like a weapon, but it seems more for show than to render a blow. He usually wears a suit of armor that is colorful and ornate. His position indicates that he is riding toward some encounter, more likely a joust than a fight.

KNIGHT of WANDS.

## UPRIGHT

Knights are messengers and travelers, and the Knight of Wands is bringing good news concerning work or social activities. His glad tidings may relate to almost any anticipated happy event— a journey or vacation, a change of residence or job, an engagement or marriage. If this card represents a specific person, it will refer to a young man who is a relative or friend with the same qualities as the King and Queen, who are his parents in the royal family. It also indicates that the person bearing the message can be trusted and is faithful.

## REVERSED

Even when reversed, the Wands aren't particularly negative, but the reversed Knight can indicate a delay in a message or paperwork you have been expecting. A trip may be canceled because of bad weather or an engagement or wedding postponed, or even broken off. The reversed Knight can represent separation from people, places, or situations.

# PAGE OF WANDS

The Page of Wands shows a youth, generally facing sideways and holding a tall staff before him with both hands, perhaps leaning on it. His attitude is expectant but casual. He is wearing garb similar to that of the rest of the royal court, but because he is a youth he may wear short pants. Some contemporary decks depict the Page as a girl or an androgynous figure.

PAGE of WANDS.

## UPRIGHT

The Page of Wands represents a message of importance to your current project or situation, usually affecting work although it may be of a social nature. The information is positive. If the card represents a person in your life, it could be a younger relative or friend, an apprentice, student, or assistant. This Page is an enthusiastic adventurer and may be interested in international travel, foreign cultures and people, the arts, or philosophic projects.

## REVERSED

When reversed, the Page of Wands represents a delay, which could cause trouble. Something you were expecting might not arrive on time or a mix-up may occur. Or the Page may bring a message of unwelcome news that causes some disruption in your life or requires you to travel to put things right. If this Page represents a person, he is someone not to be trusted, or who conveys false or misleading information. Be on guard.

The Ace of Wands in the Waite and some other decks shows a hand emerging from a cloud, firmly grasping a heavy yet elegantly shaped stick that is vaguely phallic in design. Out of the wand, or club, new shoots are growing. The disembodied hand holds the Wand so that it points upward. Some decks picture only a wand, often one that is large and elaborate, like a ruler's scepter or a magician's ceremonial tool.

ACE of WANDS.

## UPRIGHT

This Ace indicates the beginning of an enterprise, usually involving business, the arts, or finance. It shows that you have planted the seeds for a new birth—possibly a creative or money-making idea. You are now free from restraints that have hampered you in the past, enabling you to express yourself successfully, take on a new role, or forge a new identity through your work.

## REVERSED

The Ace of Wands reversed indicates that the process of creating a new identity or the start of a new endeavor has not yet manifested. It's still in the planning stages. You may be experiencing delays, or you might have to rethink your plans and make adjustments. You have a sense of your potential to do something new but could be hesitating because of lack of resources or confidence.

The Two of Wands is an ambiguous card. It shows that a second, perhaps unexpected, factor is entering into the situation at hand, something for which your plans have not allowed. There is an element of surprise. Sometimes this card indicates a choice must be made, which could be related to your work or a creative endeavor.

### UPRIGHT

You are saying "Yes" to a new enterprise with the expectation that you will achieve ownership, wealth, and good fortune. You've started something and are awaiting results. You may, however, have to deal with some unforeseen problems or encounter unexpected obstacles and opposition, such as a bank loan not coming through, a partner defecting, or a loss of support you were counting on. Sometimes this card can indicate a need to alter your course.

### REVERSED

This position suggests you may be in for a surprise, perhaps a nasty one. Nonetheless, you are affirming your new self-concept whether you have told others about it or not. Whether the surprise element portends good or bad will be indicated by the surrounding cards in the reading. If the Two of Wands appears with a Court card, for example, it may mean the person the Court card represents will disappoint you or make an unexpected appearance, which will change the picture.

The Three of Wands represents someone who is ready and willing to hang on to what he has achieved. You can remain calm and in control of the situation, for there is no need for impulsiveness. This is a time for taking things firmly in hand and to act in a mature and responsible manner based on your experience and common sense.

## UPRIGHT

You have consolidated your situation, business, or enterprise and now can expect financial and/or personal gain. By clearly defining the role you want to play, you are presenting a positive picture to the world. This confident attitude may draw helpful people toward you or attract beneficial circumstances. You've established a solid foundation for your business or occupation and can expect cooperation from others. At this point, you are clear about who you are and what you intend to achieve. Others will respond positively to you.

## REVERSED

You are doing most of the work on an internal level, clarifying your needs and formulating your sense of direction. You have resolved most of the problems connected to the situation or enterprise and negotiated the tricky bits. Now you can expect things to go smoothly when you do go public with your ideas.

This is an extremely positive card, indicating that your efforts to establish a project, business, or other endeavor are successful. Your position is secure and comfortable. Now you can relax and enjoy life. It's a time of respite and rejoicing.

## UPRIGHT

You are enjoying pleasure and prosperity, reaping the rewards you have earned. Your finances are in good shape, and you are in harmony with your environment and the people in it. You've shown the world who you truly are and what you can achieve. It's a time for celebration and good times.

## REVERSED

As this is a very positive card, the reversed position means only that you are celebrating your good fortune in a quiet way. You may be expanding your property holdings or creative output without fanfare. Financial gains may be more modest than if the card were upright, but you are satisfied with your accomplishments and the sense of having done a job well. Your public image, your relationships with others, and your sense of self are favorable.

# FIVE OF WANDS

The Five of Wands is about competition in economic, social, or career areas. It signifies the mad scramble for money and power, success and recognition, with concomitant excesses of greed and corruption. This card represents struggle in the marketplace. It can also indicate that you are involved in ego battles with other people in your workplace or the social arena. Often the image on the card shows five men fighting among themselves, using their staves as weapons.

## UPRIGHT

New factors moving into the situation are demanding that you change, adapt, and grow. Life's not as simple as it was. New competition has moved into the neighborhood—or the industry—and you have to put forth a lot more effort to keep what you have gained in terms of money, status, and material goods. Depending on the rest of the reading and how you handle the challenges facing you, you could either suffer hardship and loss or go on to greater success and prosperity.

## REVERSED

When the Five of Wands is reversed, you must challenge yourself to change and adapt to different and difficult circumstances. The new competition may be cutthroat, even dishonest or underhanded. There could be litigation to resolve disputes, and your public image may suffer. Don't get involved in questionable or risky practices at this time and be careful whom you trust.

# SIX OF WANDS

The Six of Wands represents triumphing over adversity. A card of victory, it indicates good news and success. You've met the challenges to your position, work, or reputation and come through with flying colors.

## UPRIGHT

Victory is at hand. You have overcome or conquered the opposition. Past self-doubt has been resolved, and you are in the process of winning some significant battles. You can expect to succeed and have your desires gratified. Gifts may be received, awards and recognition won.

## REVERSED

The hopes and wishes you have for your success are being delayed, often by factors over which you have no control. You feel frustrated and angry, ready to do battle to get things set right. You're being challenged by circumstances to take a stance about who you are and what you intend to accomplish. You may have experienced some kind of betrayal that has caused you to re-evaluate your self-image.

The Seven of Wands is about courage and determination. It indicates you are willing to fight for what you believe in and will stand your ground. Previously, you might have fallen into complacency but now you are ready to face challenges.

## UPRIGHT

Profit and gain come only after you have firmly held off your competition or enemies. You may be outnumbered, but your determination will win the day. You are discovering inner resources you hardly suspected you had and using them to overcome obstacles. Thus, you have the advantage and will eventually achieve success by sheer force of will and personality.

## REVERSED

This position signifies a time of confusion. You don't know whether to hold on or back off, but now is the time for firmness and decision. Even if you're not sure which way to go, it's one of those situations where any decision is better than none at all.

This is a card of movement, action, and excitement. Things happen rapidly, and success is assured. Follow through on what you've already put in motion and start planning new goals.

### UPRIGHT

You have shot your arrows into the air, and they are speeding toward the target. Now is a time for action, for initiating the next phase of your enterprise. This may involve air travel or other movement. It's an exciting and hopeful period when you are likely to be extremely busy. Positive things are rapidly unfolding. Establish the roles you want to play and let go of those that no longer suit you.

### REVERSED

Movement may be unwanted, stressful, or unpleasant, such as being transferred across the country when you'd rather stay put. Go with the flow, wherever it leads. Allow yourself to be open to new experiences, but be prepared—be aware of what you're getting into. Relationships—marriage, business partnerships, family—may suffer. You may be required to reprioritize your schedule to accommodate other people's needs.

The Nine of Wands represents defending your legitimate territory. Through effort and determination, you have protected what's yours, shown courage under fire, and stood your ground. This is a card of recovery. Now you are in a strong position, and success is at hand.

## UPRIGHT

Nines represent completion, and the Nine of Wands in a reading indicates that the job is done. You have had the discipline and the ability to plan well and wisely. Your relationships are developing positively, and you are moving forward with a sense of purpose and direction. If there is still opposition, your skills, strength, and courage will prevail over all opponents.

## REVERSED

You may be fighting a losing battle. If so, it's time to cut your losses and get out. Whatever it is, it is over, and if it hasn't worked out for you then go on to something else. Learn the lessons of failure—failure is but success's opposite and the wheel always turns. Get on with your life.

The Ten of Wands shows you taking up new responsibilities appropriate to the new cycle that's beginning now. These may seem burdensome, but you have the strength and character to shoulder them. You feel you can do anything at this time, even an extremely difficult task.

## UPRIGHT

Your labor may have gone for naught, or you may be carrying burdens that really don't belong to you. You feel weary, as if the whole world is on your shoulders. It's up to you to decide whether to continue carrying the heavy responsibilities you have undertaken or if other people are shirking their part and should help out. Sometimes, one member of a family or organization gets all the dirty work for the simple reason that they are willing to do it. Make sure others are doing their fair share. Ask for help if you need it; don't let pride stand in your way.

## REVERSED

The burden is lifted—sometimes unexpectedly—and there is a feeling of freedom from undue responsibilities. Either you have taken the appropriate action or are about to do so. In any case, your load has been shifted, reproportioned, or removed entirely. You are learning to delegate and take on less. Pressure and stress are reduced, and you are able to enjoy life more. Sometimes, however, depending on negative influences in the spread, you may be suffering the consequences of overload—either with ill health or burnout. You may need a recovery period.

# THE SUIT OF PENTACLES

In medieval times, the suit of Pentacles, or Coins, referred to the merchant class. These cards represented tradesmen involved in buying and selling goods, building up commerce and trade routes, sending ships around the world, and getting rich in the process. Today, Pentacles are related to money, security, material goods, and the physical world in general.

# INTERPRETING THE PENTACLES

Pentacles are often depicted as discs of gold, sometimes with a star (pentagram) or a five-sided design (pentagon) in the center. Interestingly, the pentacle is a powerful symbol in magick, used for protection against harmful influences, so there is also a suggestion that money and material resources can provide protection.

The suit of Pentacles (or Coins) has come to represent people who deal in the economy, whether captains of industry, professionals, accountants, entrepreneurs, shopkeepers, or those engaged in doing business in general. It includes bankers, lawyers, businessmen and women, stock traders—in other words, most of today's middle and upper-middle classes. Pentacles can also symbolize those who desire to upgrade themselves financially, who understand money and how it works, and who respect the power it confers. In a reading, Pentacles usually point to an increase in the finances of the querent, and can show success in business, a raise, or relief from financial difficulties.

Therefore, in general the appearance of Pentacles is a positive note on a temporal basis. As Pentacles represent the element Earth, they also indicate groundedness in the material and physical world. They can suggest concern about financial security, career, or whatever work you do as your livelihood. In some instances, Pentacles describe other types of material resources, physical capabilities, or health conditions.

# KING OF PENTACLES

The King of Pentacles is usually shown as a royal figure regally dressed and seated on a throne. In some decks, the throne is decorated with animal figures such as a lion, a bull, an eagle, or a griffin (signifying the four fixed signs of the zodiac). He may or may not be crowned, but he appears comfortable with the power money confers. Generally the King holds a single coin upright in one hand and a scepter in the other.

KING of PENTACLES.

## UPRIGHT

This King represents a mature man who is not only wealthy but also courageous. He is a solid citizen, reputable, dependable, and kind to others. He symbolizes worldly power in a positive sense and is experienced in handling money matters. His stability is a major factor, making him someone who can provide reliable counsel on matters of money, property, and security.

If the King represents an actual person, he is likely to be well-disposed toward the querent—possibly he is a corporate head where the person works, or a banker from whom the querent is soliciting a loan. If the King is not an actual person, then his appearance indicates that the querent is engaged in some worldly enterprise that will meet with success.

## REVERSED

Some people consider this King reversed to be an extremely negative symbol, representing danger or an unwise business move. Others view the card as a warning to be aware of the small print in any contracts being negotiated. The King can also indicate unfair competition or shady business practices.

The Queen of Pentacles is a benevolent figure with a regal and kindly bearing, sometimes shown holding the Pentacle or coin in her lap and gazing fondly down at it. She may also be pictured standing, leaning against an ornate throne or chair. Like the King, her throne is often decorated with animal figures. She is someone who understands and respects money as a tool but does not worship it.

QUEEN of PENTACLES.

## UPRIGHT

This Queen represents a generous woman who is also an excellent manager in practical and financial areas. She may be a sensual woman who is at home in her body and enjoys her creature comforts. As an advisor, she favors the querent or will at least be fair. She is pragmatic and realistic and wants to see that the money she distributes produces tangible results. If the card doesn't represent a person, it shows a harvest after much labor, security, the acquisition of wisdom through experience, and prudent use of wealth.

## REVERSED

In the reversed position, this Queen may represent someone who will try to block your efforts. She could be merely indifferent, or actively hostile. She might be a superficial person who only pretends to want to help you. Or the price of her help might be too high; she wants to control everything. She may lack confidence and try to compensate by a display of her wealth, or she may be hiding a lack of money. If this card does not represent a person, it describes a situation where caution is due and advises you to be careful whom you trust.

This Knight brings news concerning money, usually good news. He is typically depicted on horseback, facing sideways, wearing armor, and holding the Pentacle before him as if offering it to someone. Unlike the Knight of Wands who is on a charging horse, the Knight of Pentacles's horse is at parade rest, calm and stable. He is poised on the edge of adventure or travel.

**KNIGHT of PENTACLES.**

## UPRIGHT

If this Knight represents a person, it's someone with the spirit of adventure, but who is practical and materially minded. He is good at performing any task set for him, but not likely to be a self-starter. If the card does not signify a person, it suggests a situation involving arrivals and/or departures. You may quit a job for a more lucrative one elsewhere, move to another locale for financial or work-related reasons, or experience other changes in your life relative to money, possessions, or security.

## REVERSED

The Knight reversed brings an unwelcome message about money, often a loss of some kind, a disappointment, or frustration due to an unforeseen delay. Existing plans may have to be aborted; delays could cause failure. If the card represents a person, he may be a young man who is unemployed or uninterested in employment. If it's not a person, this Knight shows a situation where waste, inertia, and problems with money exist.

# PAGE OF PENTACLES

The Page of Pentacles is often shown as a youth standing in a countryside. He is holding the Pentacle before him, as if admiring it. His attitude suggests that he desires money or wants to achieve the means to gain it, perhaps through education. Sometimes called the card of the student or scholar, the Page of Pentacles shows one who is so intent on his lessons that he misses everything else going on around him. In some contemporary decks, the Page is pictured as a girl or androgynous figure.

PAGE of PENTACLES.

## UPRIGHT

The Page of Pentacles indicates good news regarding the acquisition of money or material goods. His appearance suggests someone who is intelligent, refined, sensitive to the arts, and appreciative of the good life. Ambitious and determined, he is goal-oriented. If he does not represent a person, this card indicates your own worldly ambitions and/or a message concerning them.

## REVERSED

This Page in the reversed position reflects someone who is lazy, unmotivated, or uninterested in furthering himself through education or work. If the card does not represent a person, it may indicate bad news concerning money matters. It can also refer to some sort of disappointment such as failing an exam, not getting into the college of your choice, or not being hired for a job. More effort and focus are needed.

# ACE OF PENTACLES

The Ace of Pentacles often depicts a large Pentacle as the central image on the card. In the Waite deck, a hand is coming out of a cloud holding the Pentacle in its palm. Other decks illustrate the coin in a decorative manner, sometimes as a shield. The Ace of Pentacles is the card of new success, new money, new enterprise, resources, ambition, opportunity, and material attainment. In some cases, it can also represent physical or health-related benefits.

ACE of PENTACLES.

## UPRIGHT

This Ace is extremely positive, predicting success for some new enterprise you are starting. You are planting the seeds for a new venture involving the acquisition of money or financial security. The Ace is a strong indication of prosperity coming to you. Be open to receive the benefits it promises.

## REVERSED

This Ace in the reversed position indicates that your new venture is still in the idea stage. You are laying the groundwork to achieve a greater level of security and prosperity. Your material gain will come, but it is being delayed, and you must be patient and persistent. Don't get discouraged.

The Two of Pentacles suggests either money coming from two sources or having to juggle finances to make ends meet. In some cases, it shows a financial or business partnership. It is a positive card indicating good fortune and enjoyment. You may be experiencing financial difficulty, but it won't last. Better times lie ahead.

## UPRIGHT

A message about money could be on its way to you, probably in written form. You are still in the stage of deciding which of two different options to choose. Perhaps you are concerned about financial issues and may be holding down more than one job, or moonlighting to make extra money. It's time to make a choice and stick with it even if you aren't sure of the outcome.

## REVERSED

You may be experiencing financial difficulties while pretending that all is well. You are juggling not only sources of income but also options for change. This isn't the right time to make a change. Hang in there until the right moment presents itself. You need to overcome doubt and have faith in yourself.

# THREE OF PENTACLES

The Three of Pentacles is the card of the craftsman, someone who has already developed skill in a profession or trade. It's time to turn these skills to profit, and success is assured. The Three of Pentacles usually shows you are planning and conferring about a future action, such as cooperating in a business venture.

## UPRIGHT

You are acquiring marketable skills, preparing yourself for action in the world. You might be a recent graduate or have gone back to school to upgrade your skills or change your career. You are enterprising and may be interested in some particular area of commerce, or a specific trade or business. You can anticipate a rise in prestige and earnings. This card can also indicate a payback period when you demonstrate your abilities and begin to reap the rewards of your efforts. Or you could receive money that's owed to you.

## REVERSED

You aren't making the effort to acquire the new skills you need in today's changing marketplace. You may be stuck in a job you really don't like but lack the confidence or ambition to strike out and change things for the better. You need to get going—thought without action is invalid.

# FOUR OF PENTACLES

The Four of Pentacles indicates a security-conscious person who is holding tight to money and material possessions. You may fear that loss is in the offing and are trying to prepare yourself by closely guarding what you have. Or you may simply be overly cautious and conservative in financial areas.

## UPRIGHT

You are hanging on to something—either your possessions or a situation—in a stubborn and inflexible manner. Fear of change may be involved, or you may merely be comfortable where you are. Your fixed attitude, however, may be limiting you and blocking new opportunities for success and happiness.

## REVERSED

You may be trying to make something happen prematurely, or you are holding on too tightly to current circumstances. Perhaps you are quarreling with someone over money, such as in a divorce proceeding. You need to loosen up and have more trust in the universe to provide.

Of all the Pentacles, this is the only one with a basic negative connotation. It suggests financial losses, business problems, or material lack. It can also indicate that spiritual bankruptcy is at the root of this unfavorable condition. In some instances, this card can show that your priorities are spiritual, not financial or worldly.

## UPRIGHT

This Five is a warning that money may soon be very tight, that losses may ensue from ill-advised investments, or that support you had counted on won't be forthcoming, such as a grant, legacy, or job. In some cases, it advises you to ask for help—from other people or the universe.

## REVERSED

You are being advised to get your house in order financially. Cut your losses any way you can to avoid further deterioration of your finances; if you are in debt, which you probably are, focus on getting it cleared out. Be extremely careful of any future investments. Don't take risks at this time.

This Six shows that past financial problems have been resolved. You can afford a charitable act because your income is steady and your security is stable. You are in a balanced position concerning income and outflow. You are using your prosperity to help others. Because Sixes represent give and take, this card can also indicate a business partnership or shared financial responsibility.

## UPRIGHT

Good things are coming to you and going out from you, in material terms. You are experiencing abundance, prosperity, and personal gratification. You may be in a position to support a good cause, perhaps by contributing financially to people who are struggling upward. This card can also represent philanthropic projects or providing work for other people.

## REVERSED

You need to recoup after a period of loss and confusion. You want to help others, but you don't have the means, and that makes you unhappy. You may be required to find a pattern that will create a sense of security for you so that you can find peace of mind.

The Seven of Pentacles is about receiving the benefits that are due to you, realizing the legitimate gain that you have earned by your own hard work. Like a farmer harvesting crops that he has nurtured through bad weather, you are reaping what you've sown. The harvest may still be a ways off, however, so keep tending your fields.

## UPRIGHT

You've put in the time and effort and paid your dues. Now you will gain in your business or other enterprise. Not only that, but you also feel great satisfaction from a job well done. Growth and good fortune are yours, well earned.

## REVERSED

You are experiencing disappointment or failure in some enterprise. Financial difficulties, usually the result of an unwise investment or a loan unpaid, may be causing you concern. It's a time to adjust your own attitudes toward how you use your money and look into how you yourself are responsible.

# EIGHT OF PENTACLES

The Eight is a card of craftsmanship and conscientious work. It suggests developing and applying your skills in a productive manner. You know what you want and how to go about achieving it. Be sincere and persevere, and your efforts will succeed. A business or project will prosper as a result of refining your craft or improving your processes. A new venture augurs success because you are training yourself intensively with a clear goal in mind.

## UPRIGHT

You are integrating old skills into a new form, or you are adding new skills. You've tried various means of making your living, and you are now finalizing how you want to use your personal resources to fulfill your needs and expand. Your sureness of purpose guarantees success. Your craftsmanship will be rewarded by increased income, opportunity, and respect.

## REVERSED

When this card is reversed, there is an indication that you have not mastered the necessary skills to achieve your goals. You may desire to begin some new enterprise, but a lack of ambition, ability, or clarity prevents your success. More effort or education may be necessary.

The Nine of Pentacles suggests independence from financial concerns and worries. You receive abundance from proper management in business or financial affairs. This card says you've arrived, accomplished your goals, and now feel secure.

## UPRIGHT

You have integrated the factors of your life into a secure base. Now you are enjoying money, resources, and physical energy as a smooth combined flow. There is plenty all around you—material well-being, order, safety, and success.

## REVERSED

Your security is shaky, and you may be dependent on someone else—perhaps a spouse or relative—for your financial well-being. Circumstances may have caused you to lose your independence. Figure out how to regain what you've lost.

The Ten of Pentacles is a happy card, indicating a solid and secure life, both in business and with your family. Your work and planning have paid off, and you are enjoying the fruits of your labor.

## UPRIGHT

You are emphasizing home and family at this point, now that you have a secure income to support them. You may be planning to build a new home, or buy a second vacation home. Family matters are at the forefront, and you have the leisure to concentrate on personal affairs. In some cases, this card can represent marrying into money or receiving an inheritance.

## REVERSED

You may be so established at this point that you are stagnating. Maybe you have retired comfortably and are just sitting around watching TV. You need to activate some growth in your life to avoid boredom. Take up a hobby, start a new business, do charity work, or teach others your skills.

# THE SUIT OF SWORDS

In early Tarot decks, Swords represented the knighthood, or noble houses, which ruled absolutely by the power of the sword. Yet, this class was also aware of its obligations to protect the people they governed—the obligation of the noble class to better those under their control. Today the Swords show states of mind and mental activity, communication, psychological matters, and spiritual issues.

# INTERPRETING THE SWORDS

The Swords represent events, conditions, situations, or attitudes that may be difficult or challenging. However, as a result, they also represent the growth and development of the conscious mind. When Swords appear in a reading, you may be experiencing stress or problems, but these are making you think.

An old Chinese proverb says, "Life is pain. Pain makes you think. Thinking makes you wise. And wisdom makes life endurable." This is the point of view that the Swords represent.

The suffering associated with the Swords can also be the result of overanalyzing situations. In our modern society, where left-brain logic is favored over right-brain intuition and feeling, Swords can represent the alienation that comes from cutting yourself off from your inner self.

The Swords are often depicted as unsheathed double-bladed sabers, sometimes as daggers or the magician's tool known as an athame. Although usually shown as battle swords, they have a quality of power and authority wielded for some purpose other than physical fighting. Some writers interpret the Swords as totally negative; others see a spiritual side to the Swords as well as the obstacles, pain, and difficulties sometimes associated with them. This is because we often come to a spiritual path through or after intense suffering of some kind, be it physical, mental, psychological, or emotional.

# KING OF SWORDS

The King of Swords is a somewhat stern figure who is in absolute command, but who can be trusted to be fair in his judgment and decisions. He is usually pictured enthroned, armored, helmeted, and crowned, a combination of symbols that suggests not only power and authority, but also a willingness to use it forcefully if necessary. The suit of Swords corresponds to the element of Air. Therefore, his appearance often has to do with your mental processes.

KING of SWORDS.

## UPRIGHT

This King represents a man of great strength and authority. If he stands for a person, it is someone who is involved with mental work, such as a researcher, lawyer, teacher, someone in the communications field, or a military officer. As such, he is a good counselor with acute mental dexterity. He has a gift for thinking clearly and rapidly, and he is able to express his thoughts with considerable eloquence. If this King is not a person, he represents a situation in which mental and communication skills are called for. When he appears, you may be on the verge of a spiritual breakthrough and are ready to communicate it.

## REVERSED

When reversed, this King shows the negative qualities of the Air signs—fickleness, using words as rapiers to wound, gossiping, superficiality, playing one person against the other, or rigidity of opinions. If he does not signify a person, he can represent a situation in which the people around you are antagonistic to your ideas or your spiritual quest. You may have to keep these matters to yourself and not advertise them to those who are unsympathetic.

The Queen of Swords is the female counterpart of the King, except that she represents the intuitive and creative side of the mental processes. A mature woman who sits on an ornate throne and wears beautiful robes, she holds her sword in one hand and reaches out with the other in a gesture suggesting permission to rise and come forward. She is a formidable figure with power and authority, either in the mental world or in the spiritual realm.

QUEEN of SWORDS.

## UPRIGHT

The Queen of Swords may represent a single or independent woman with authority and power. Often she is someone with keen intellectual or communicative abilities. In some instances, this card may indicate someone who has endured emotional loss and separation, perhaps as a result of a divorce or death. If she describes a person, she is strong-willed and has the ability to cope with her loss and go on with her life. If she does not represent a person, this Queen can indicate that the querent is going through a difficult experience, which will open new vistas if she uses it for positive growth.

## REVERSED

When this Queen is reversed, the person she represents is not dealing well with whatever loss is involved. There may be sadness, withdrawal, or mourning beyond reasonable limits. If the card does not stand for a person, it can represent a situation in which the querent is bogged down emotionally, wallowing in pain, letting her heart rule her head. Other cards in the spread will indicate the way out of the dilemma.

# KNIGHT OF SWORDS

The Knight of Swords is often shown leaning forward on a fully charging horse, his sword held upright and forward as if he is ready to encounter the enemy. He is definitely on the attack and by his expression he expects to win the battle. He can represent a person who is overly aggressive or argumentative, who lives in attack mode. Or he can mean that you are aggressively pursuing a lifestyle that will allow you to live out your own philosophical ideals.

KNIGHT of SWORDS.

## UPRIGHT

As a messenger, the Knight of Swords may bring bad news that relates to you personally or to someone close to you. Some kind of conflict is at hand, usually of a mental nature. There could be violent differences of opinion around you, with angry messages being sent and received. Or if this Knight is not a person, you may be so focused on your intellectual pursuits that you are neglecting other facets of your life. You may be expressing your ideas too forcefully and are antagonizing the opposition. Diplomacy may be called for in a situation.

## REVERSED

When reversed, this Knight loses his aggressiveness and becomes passive about a situation that requires action. He suggests you are delaying doing what is necessary, perhaps neglecting paperwork or communication. There could be serious repercussions from withholding information. If this card is not a person, it can indicate that you are mentally closed off from a situation that desperately needs attention and is thereby creating bad feeling and opposition.

# PAGE OF SWORDS

The Page of Swords is about risk on a mental or spiritual level. It might mean you are taking up some new line of thought or study. Many decks depict a youth standing, looking over his shoulder away from the sword he holds. He seems a bit unsure of his ability to wield the weapon although he tries to appear as if he can easily defeat any enemy. He usually wears a short garment, leather or padded cloth, instead of armor. Some contemporary decks show the Page as a girl or androgynous figure.

PAGE of SWORDS.

## UPRIGHT

As a messenger, this Page brings news of problems and difficulties, perhaps relating to a younger person you know. An offspring may have failed college exams or be in trouble with the law. An element of experimentation is indicated here—either you or someone else is taking a risk or behaving in a risky manner that might cause problems. The Page is motivated by unconventional activity, which can cause strife. Overconfidence or the ignorance of youth might also get this person into trouble.

## REVERSED

The reversed Page is having trouble getting it together. Although this young person is attractive and charming—eager, confident, clever, active—he isn't strictly on the up and up. This Page could represent someone who is sponging off others, maybe parents or friends. Or it could indicate someone who is anxious or capable of spiteful action. Insecurity lies at the root of this person's actions.

Like all of the Aces, the Ace of Swords indicates a new beginning. Most decks depict an upright sword, sometimes crowned at the tip. In the Waite deck, a disembodied hand coming out of clouds holds the Sword. The Sword and crown are decorated with living vegetation—vines, flowers, leaves, fruit. This Ace indicates a triumph over difficulties through the use of mental means or spiritual growth. It is emblematic of a major breakthrough.

ACE of SWORDS.

## UPRIGHT

A brand new lifestyle is coming into being for you. You have achieved this opportunity by dint of will and using your mental faculties at a high level. Prosperity, recognition, new development—especially spiritual growth—are sure to follow in the wake of your new direction in life. This Ace signals a birth—of an idea, an enterprise, or a child. You now are in a position of power with the possibility of manifesting your philosophy in a new way.

## REVERSED

As this is an extremely positive card, the reversed position only indicates delays or glitches. What you planned for on the mental plane may not come into manifestation on the physical plane as quickly as you had hoped, and this may be causing frustration and tension.

The Waite deck shows a blindfolded woman holding two swords crossed over her breasts with a crescent Moon above and the ocean behind her. The card represents a situation in which it appears impossible to move forward. Because you can't figure out with logic or intellect how to proceed, you must rely on blind faith that the universe will handle things.

## UPRIGHT

This card indicates stasis. You may be maintaining the situation in a state of balance by ignoring the underlying tension that exists. This is an uncomfortable position to be in, but you aren't ready to do anything about it yet. You need to speak up and communicate about the circumstances involved. For instance, it can represent a couple who really do not get along but are putting up a perfect façade to the outside world. Eventually, however, change must take place for the continued tension is unbearable. Choice is available. Remove the blindfold and look honestly at the situation.

## REVERSED

When the Two of Swords appears reversed, it exacerbates the stasis, except that the person actually feels helpless to make the necessary changes. If a husband and wife are at odds, one party may be unwilling to admit to the truth of the situation, making discourse impossible. This may result in deceit or disloyalty, lying or duplicity.

The Three of Swords is a card of severance, signifying separation and sorrow, perhaps the end of a love relationship. However, there is the sense that the separation or breakup was needed. A relationship or alliance had outworn its usefulness, and, although there is sorrow or regret, the end result is positive. This card can also mean you feel isolated and cut off from something you love—a way of life, your home and family, a philosophy, pursuit, or job.

## UPRIGHT

You are feeling the pain of separation right now, quite possibly in the area of love. Sometimes this card can signify a love triangle. A third party has entered into the formerly stable situation and caused the breakup, but it was ready to happen anyway. It's time to let go. Whatever has died must be allowed to disintegrate within your psychic structure. Don't try to hold on to the past.

## REVERSED

You are taking this separation too much to heart and not thinking clearly about the truth of the situation. You may be blaming someone else instead of acknowledging that you were a party to the breakup. You may be suffering depression over the situation, unable or unwilling to pull yourself together and get on with your life. Try to keep a clear head and don't get bogged down with what might have been.

# FOUR OF SWORDS

The Four of Swords is a card of respite after the sorrow or misfortune of the Three. It represents rest and recuperation, of working on your problems quietly and with faith. You feel the need for introspection and solitude, a necessary period of aloneness and contemplation to understand what happened and why.

## UPRIGHT

You have been in pain, but now you are in the first stage of recovery, whether from emotional upheaval or physical illness. You are resting and taking the time out to think things through and plan your next moves more wisely. This is the calm after the storm, and you may want to retreat from other people and the world. During this time, think, plan, and re-evaluate what you had been doing before the crisis. It's time to get your inner house in order.

## REVERSED

You are not allowing yourself the rest and respite you need, and if you continue this way you may make yourself ill. Everyone needs a period of calm and quiet in the wake of any kind of major disruption. Refusing to make time to recuperate, both mentally and emotionally, will only worsen the situation. Take heed and take time out.

# FIVE OF SWORDS

The Five of Swords suggests the double-edged nature of the sword. One edge signifies defeat, misfortune, betrayal, and loss; the other suggests learning to accept the boundaries we all must face and live with. Fives are about adjusting, and this Five indicates you are adjusting to some kind of change brought on by distress or loss. It's an uncomfortable process but a necessary one.

## UPRIGHT

Change is part of life, and the more you resist it, the more difficult you make things for yourself. Whatever needs to be changed—your lifestyle, your philosophy, your inner beliefs about yourself—now is the time to get to work and bring those changes into your daily life.

## REVERSED

Your losses have hit you hard, and you are in a state of great unhappiness. You feel hurt and betrayed, angry and discouraged. This is a time of agony, but only you can get yourself out of it. You may feel confused about why the crisis occurred, but deep down you are already aware of the reasons. You just don't want to face them.

# SIX OF SWORDS

The Six of Swords indicates that you are moving away from past troubles, putting them behind you. It marks the beginning of a new phase after a time of upheaval. You have stabilized yourself and are enjoying a new peace of mind. This is the calm after the storm—a period of smooth sailing with relatively few problems ahead.

## UPRIGHT

This is a time of integration—or reintegration. Harmony and ease prevail. New people you can trust come into your life. After some intense suffering, you now feel optimistic and balanced. This card can also indicate a move or a journey over water. The destination may be unknown, or the effects of the move may be uncertain, but luck is on your side, and any change you make will go smoothly.

## REVERSED

As this is a positive card, the reversed position simply means delays, or that the harmony you are experiencing is internal rather than being expressed externally. You may have come to a new way of thinking about your life, or you may be affirming your old beliefs and attitudes, finding a path that's comfortable for you.

When the Seven of Swords shows up, it urges caution in all dealings. Surreptitious action or indirect communications may be occurring. Nothing is quite what it seems to be, and you have to use your wit to achieve your aims. Be wary of overconfidence. You may appear to be on top now, but imprudence could still do you in.

## UPRIGHT

You have got the upper hand over a tricky situation, but you still need to exercise caution in handling your affairs. Discretion and discrimination are required, as are diplomacy and evasive tactics. You may not like this oblique approach, but you'll be more likely to achieve success this way.

## REVERSED

When the Seven of Swords appears reversed, it emphasizes all of the previously mentioned attributes but includes the possibility of deception. Maintain caution and vigilance in all things during this period. Stay open-minded and flexible so that you can respond to changes speedily. You may be experimenting with different plans of action, getting various points of view.

The tension of the Eight of Swords is related to that of the Two, except that the Two indicates denial while the Eight suggests the querent is conscious of the choices available. Despite this, you feel trapped—either unable or unwilling to make a choice, therefore stuck in a painful state. You are your own worst enemy.

## UPRIGHT

Most writers view this as an extremely negative card. In the Waite deck, a bound and blindfolded woman is surrounded by eight swords stuck into the sand around her, like a barrier. The card describes a situation that causes great unhappiness, but you are not without resources to change matters. The bad situation is temporary and, if the card falls in the "future" position, the problem can even be avoided.

## REVERSED

This card reversed is a warning that what is already wrong can get worse, or that a difficult situation is approaching. Make sure all your affairs are in the best possible order. If you've been putting off paying your taxes, or getting insurance, or settling some legal matter, take care of it promptly. Your well-being depends on using your head and preparing for emergencies and unexpected calamities.

The Nine of Swords shows extreme anxiety, nightmares, tension, unhappiness, and regrets over past mistakes or misfortunes. When it appears, the querent is in an unhappy and tense state of mind whether or not the facts bear out the fear. Thus the suffering associated with this card may be mostly in your mind.

## UPRIGHT

The Nine of Swords indicates that the querent is troubled by bad dreams or horrible fantasies. You may not even know where these are coming from, but deep-rooted or repressed issues are trying to surface so you can recognize and resolve them. Extreme mental torture may result as you are forced to change your attitudes and beliefs by crisis circumstances. This is not all bad, however, no matter how painful it seems. Remember that Nine is the number of completion. Thus, this card indicates that the changes you are being required to make forecast a better future.

## REVERSED

When the Nine of Swords is reversed, it shows intense mental anguish. It's time to examine belief systems that no longer apply to your life and that are standing in the way of your progress. You are suffering because you refuse to face the cause of your problems. Honesty is called for to gain the insight you need to resolve the situation.

Although the Ten of Swords is another difficult card, its appearance marks the beginning of the end of a period of trials and tribulations. It also signifies the beginning of an entirely new cycle. For the new cycle to come in, you have to clear away the debris of the old cycle now ending, and often this process is painful. Extreme stress and exhaustion may accompany the appearance of this card. You need to stop worrying.

### UPRIGHT

When the Ten of Swords appears upright, it suggests that you need to make a clean break from the past and all its attendant pain and suffering. Whether this means a divorce, quitting a job, changing careers, moving across the country, or changing a traditional belief system, make the break and make it cleanly, leaving no loose ends. It's time to do away with previous illusions that have clouded your vision.

### REVERSED

When the Ten of Swords appears reversed, it is an indication that you are holding back and are reluctant to take the necessary steps to move into a new cycle. You are delaying actions or deceiving yourself about a situation. You may be making excuses for yourself or someone else to maintain the status quo, but you are only prolonging your agony. Make a choice, even if it's the wrong one.

# THE SUIT OF CUPS

The Cups in medieval times represented the clergy, whose influence in the society was second only to the nobility. In fact, it was common practice for the second or third son of a noble house to enter the Church. Although the clergy often fell short of its obligations, the local priests were frequently good people who used available resources to help their flocks. For this reason, the suit of Cups has come to represent love, happiness, companionship, compassion, and benign influences.

# INTERPRETING THE CUPS

In a broader interpretation, the Cups describe emotions, love, romance, social relationships, congenial situations, culture, comfort, intuition, and the unconscious. The love shown by these cards is not just romantic love, but friendship and love of one's fellow humans as well. Kindness, compassion, and geniality are depicted in the imagery of this suit. Thus, the Cups are almost always considered positive, and if there are negative factors in the reading, a Cups card will mitigate the bad omen, help to make a situation better, or point the way to a solution. The symbol for the Cups is a happy one. In most decks they are pictured as large, beautiful, often ornate vessels or chalices. Sometimes they appear double-ended as if they could be filled from either side.

The King of Cups has a loving demeanor. He is a mature man, usually pictured seated on a throne, often with water in the background. In the Waite deck, his crown is more like an elaborate hat than a bejeweled regal headpiece, suggesting that he stands with rather than above his subjects. This King's expression is benign, his attitude relaxed and nonthreatening.

KING of CUPS.

## UPRIGHT

This King indicates a man who is kindly disposed—a benevolent father figure, who may represent your own father or someone who fills that role for you. Whether as a friend, advisor, or lover, he is utterly trustworthy and dependent, and he can be relied upon to come through for you when you need him. Most interpretations consider this King to be a man of culture, knowledgeable about and interested in the arts, possibly himself a creative type. If the King does not represent an actual person, he indicates a situation that is favorable, especially if it is an artistic pursuit.

## REVERSED

Your involvement with some kind of love situation is ending, but the process should not cause much pain. You have reached a phase in your life when it's time to move away from dependency on an older person—perhaps your father or a mentor or teacher—and strike out on your own. It is also possible that this King reversed represents someone who is trying to get rid of you for some reason, romantic or otherwise. You need to let go and, if necessary, mourn the passing of something that was good once but is now over.

# QUEEN OF CUPS

The Queen of Cups is a beautiful and benevolent figure. The Cup she holds is an ornate chalice, and she gazes at it as if she could see visions of the future inside. She wears robes that appear to be filmy and flowing, and her crown is elaborate but graceful. Usually she is pictured with water flowing at her feet, for this suit corresponds to the Water element. An affectionate and loving woman, she is wise in the ways of the human heart. Her attitude is one of receptivity and approachability.

QUEEN of CUPS.

## UPRIGHT

The Queen of Cups can represent any kindly woman in your life. If the querent is a man, she may signify his wife or the woman he loves. She is creative, perhaps an artist, with visionary tendencies. Her psychic ability is highly developed and tends to be accurate. However, she tempers her intuitive nature with mature judgment. If this Queen does not represent a person, the situation she describes may concern a creative endeavor, relationship, or circumstances with a positive emotional tone.

## REVERSED

This Queen reversed can indicate a love relationship gone sour, or someone who is having trouble expressing emotion. If the card represents a person, it can be a dishonest advisor. Be careful whom you trust with your secrets and your emotional life. If the card represents the querent, it can mean that you are playing with possible dangerous psychic matters you don't understand.

# KNIGHT OF CUPS

Portrayed as a handsome young man, usually sitting upright on a white horse in parade or dressage position, he holds the Cup straight out in front of him. His helmet may be winged, a symbol of the messenger. In this case, the message he brings is of love or good tidings. Usually depicted in an outdoor setting, sometimes with water under the horse's hooves, this Knight is armored only lightly. He's a lover, not a fighter.

KNIGHT of CUPS.

## UPRIGHT

The Knight of Cups is bringing you a message about love, or he may represent your true love—the knight on the white horse! His appearance indicates you are deeply involved in an emotional situation, to the point where little else matters. You may be awaiting this message—such as a declaration of love or a proposal of marriage—with such anticipation that everything else seems insignificant. All other relationships pale when compared with this one. If the Knight does not represent a lover, he is certainly a friend, honest, intelligent, and willing to aid you.

## REVERSED

The message you hope for has been delayed or may never arrive. The relationship you yearn for may be based on deceit or superficiality on the other person's side. You may be obsessing about someone who really doesn't care that much about you and who will never make a commitment, even if he has led you to believe he is sincere. This person is fickle, likes to flirt, but belongs to the "love 'em and leave 'em" school of romance.

The Page of Cups usually shows a young man in decorative short garb wearing an elaborate hat. His attitude is relaxed and open, and he seems well pleased with himself. In the Waite deck, he holds the Cup out in one hand—a fish, symbol of the Water element, peeks out of it. It's as though he magically produced the fish like a rabbit out of a hat, and he seems to expect approval. Some decks depict the Page as a girl or androgynous figure.

**PAGE of CUPS.**

## UPRIGHT

This Page signifies a young person, male or female—possibly a son, daughter, or a younger sibling—who is bringing you a message about love. It might mean an engagement or a wedding—some situation that holds an inherent emotional risk. The circumstances may be exciting yet scary at the same time, as with a sudden elopement. Often the Page suggests naiveté or vulnerability, especially in matters of the heart. If the card represents the querent, it says you have already decided to take an emotional risk and aren't interested in being dissuaded. You are willing to give it your all and feel things will work out.

## REVERSED

The Page reversed shows a fishy situation, something you should look at carefully. If the card represents a person, there may be deceit involved—flattery for gain, an unwanted pregnancy, or secrecy in matters of the heart. Someone may be trying to seduce you, and you are blinded to the falseness of his or her intentions. Or you may be playing the role of the seducer, toying with someone's emotions. If so, take care. You might get hurt yourself.

# ACE OF CUPS

The Ace of Cups shows a single large chalice, usually with water flowing fountain-like out of it. In the Waite deck, a hand emerging from a cloud grasps the Cup as if offering it to the querent. This Ace suggests a fountain of love or the Holy Grail. Other symbols such as doves, flowers, or water motifs may decorate this card. The Ace represents a gift, in this case a gift of love, of a personal or divine nature.

ACE of CUPS.

## UPRIGHT

The Ace of Cups indicates a new beginning—a new love or a one-on-one relationship of any kind. Previously unfelt emotions come into play now, perhaps as a result of seeing a relationship in a new way. This Ace can also herald a birth—of a child or an idea. This is a fertile time for emotional or creative growth, as this Ace symbolizes the consummation of something hoped for.

## REVERSED

When reversed, this Ace indicates delays or disappointments in love. Sometimes a new beginning doesn't develop as hoped. Difficulties in getting a new relationship or creative effort off the ground could be indicated, or something you are trying to set in motion meets unforeseen and frustrating obstacles. Perhaps this is not the right time to start something new.

# TWO OF CUPS

The Two of Cups describes a coupling of some sort—a marriage, a partnership, a union. Harmony is in the air. You may be in the honeymoon stage of a relationship or endeavor when all seems right and you think nothing can go wrong. This card can also represent a new stage of happiness and harmony in an existing relationship.

## UPRIGHT

You are moving in tandem with another person now, and all is going smoothly. Whether it is a romantic relationship or a friendship, there is plenty of accord, mutual admiration, and good will toward each other. Ordinarily, this card refers to a love match between the sexes, but it can also indicate a partnership of another sort.

## REVERSED

Fortunately, this card has such a vibration of harmony that its reversed position isn't much different from the upright one. It can suggest delays or that the relationship may have to be kept a secret for some reason.

# THREE OF CUPS

The appearance of the Three of Cups signifies that something has been brought
to completion. There is victory and success. The act of falling in love signified
by the Two of Cups may have resulted
in a baby, or a creative venture has produced a salable product. It's time for a
celebration!

## UPRIGHT

You are experiencing success and
plenty, and a time of merriment and celebration is at hand. Your feelings, which
may have been murky, are clearer now,
and you understand your emotional patterns in a positive and growth-producing
way. You're on your way now to great
things.

## REVERSED

The Three of Cups reversed remains a positive influence, except
that the gratification you are getting may be more sensual than deeply
emotional. You will still have success, but your achievements may be
in small things.

# FOUR OF CUPS

The Four of Cups represents a state of apathy and withdrawal. However, this may be a necessary rest from the hectic excitement represented by the Three. It's a time to get away by yourself and just drift and dream for a while before getting back into your daily grind.

## UPRIGHT

You are in a state of withdrawing your emotions from a situation or a person. After intense emotional involvement, you may need some space in which to be yourself. There's a feeling of let-down after build-up, as in the postpartum blues or when you have to face the daily grind of ordinary life, dealing with all the nitty-gritties of making a marriage work.

## REVERSED

You may be experiencing displeasure, disappointment, or dissatisfaction with a relationship or the way a creative project is turning out. You want to tune out to get away from your negative feelings. That's okay; it is a necessary respite to regain perspective and balance.

The Five of Cups signifies that you are brooding over past wrongs, losses, disappointments, or hurts. It symbolizes a state of mind that is dwelling on a painful past and refusing to look forward to a positive future.

## UPRIGHT

Your unhappiness is a result of your attitude, which you can change. This is a card of choice. You can continue to brood over what went wrong, or you can turn around and contemplate what can go right in the future. You don't have to be miserable unless you enjoy misery.

## REVERSED

You are in a state of indecision. There's some issue about which you are refusing to make up your mind, and you are refusing to face facts. Just because there have been past losses doesn't mean there can't be future gains. If you continue in this negative state of mind, you will only make things worse.

The Six of Cups signifies nostalgia and happy memories of time gone by. This card refers to a sentimental remembrance of things past. These pleasant and comforting memories can be used to better your future, to build on. Knowing that you have been happy in the past will enhance your ability to be happy in the future.

## UPRIGHT

You are experiencing some feelings that are connected to your past that will shed light on your future. You are feeling calm and collected about past events, putting them into perspective, and beginning to understand how they can engender fruition in the present—a future renewal.

## REVERSED

A happy card, the Six of Cups reversed suggests changes in the immediate environment that will make you feel more secure. These may involve meeting new friends or making new associations. You are developing new emotional tools that will aid you in the future—an important event is coming soon.

The Seven of Cups signifies a time of great creative potential along with the energy to make use of it. Many options are available: The difficulty is in choosing the right one. This card is about fantasy and imagination.

## UPRIGHT

You are looking at a number of possibilities now—too many to make an easy choice. With so many choices, you are living out different roles in your imagination but having a hard time deciding which to manifest in reality.

## REVERSED

You are in a state of total confusion because there's too much going on. You need a calm space where you can sort through the multiple choices confronting you. Let your feelings be your guide.

# EIGHT OF CUPS

The Eight of Cups indicates a situation where the only solution is to turn your back on it and go in another direction. What's there either isn't working as expected or isn't all that important any more. The eight neatly stacked Cups represent effort that was made in vain and now needs to be abandoned.

## UPRIGHT

You are wishing things might have been different, but, knowing they aren't, you realize that you have to let go. It's time to cut your losses and get out of the situation that has failed despite your best efforts. Unfortunately, this usually refers to a relationship that has reached such a state of deterioration that the only solution is to walk away from it.

## REVERSED

You are walking away without facing the facts behind the problem you want to escape, taking the coward's way out. Things haven't worked out as you planned and hoped, and you want to cut and run without giving the situation a second chance. If you don't, you may regret it later.

This is the best pip card in the entire Tarot deck. Called the wish card, it indicates great joy and happiness, all your dreams coming true, and getting what you wish for. It's like winning the lottery and meeting Mr. or Ms. Right all on the same day.

## UPRIGHT

Even the most negative interpreters have nothing bad to say about this card. It means success, triumph, everything you want and hope for. When the Nine of Cups appears, ask yourself, "What is it I really want?" The card's answer is that you will get it!

## REVERSED

It's hard to say anything negative about this card, even in the reverse position. The worst thing that can be said here is that if you refuse to believe in your own good fortune and take a negative attitude you can mess things up for yourself.

The Ten of Cups indicates a situation of lasting contentment, real love, domestic bliss, and complete satisfaction in all your endeavors. It symbolizes people living harmoniously together, sharing their love and their lives unconditionally. This Ten is so favorable that it can offset any negative cards in a reading.

## UPRIGHT

This card is an indication of everything that most people wish for—love and harmony, happy family life, true love and compatible companionship. It's a time of completion, of reaping the rewards of what you have sown. It does not necessarily mean wealth, but it symbolizes an abundant life in the true sense.

## REVERSED

Delays and obstacles are standing in the way of achieving the happiness you long for. Circumstances beyond your control may be the cause, and at the moment there's nothing you can do but keep a positive attitude and hold tight while waiting for them to change, which they will.

### PART 3

# PERFORMING
# TAROT READINGS

# HOW TO DO READINGS

Now that you've studied the cards of the Major and Minor Arcana and are familiar with their meanings it's time to try and perform a Tarot card reading. Whether you choose to do readings for yourself or for others, to get advice about a pressing concern or for general guidance and personal growth, recognize that you are dealing with a power no one fully understands. Respect that power absolutely. Also remember in terms of the Tarot that your skill improves with practice, so don't feel dismayed if your first readings aren't perfect; the more familiar you become with your cards, the more accurate your readings will become.

# FOCUS AND ATTITUDE ARE KEY

Many factors affect the accuracy and clarity of a reading. The state of mind of the person for whom the reading is being done will profoundly influence a Tarot reading. If the querent doesn't take it seriously, or is skeptical, her doubt can set up a barrier between her rational mind and her intuition. If a querent is distracted, confused, or unclear about what he wants to know, the answers he receives from the cards will be garbled or vague.

## YOUR APPROACH TO THE CARDS

The more urgent your need to know is, the more likely you are to get a direct, definitive answer. That's because your entire consciousness is focused on the matter at hand, rather than being split up into several different areas. Your subconscious, Higher Self, spirit guides, and other levels of being long to make a connection with you and to impart their wisdom in ways that will help you. Most of us don't communicate very well with the different parts of ourselves. The Tarot provides a tool for opening up those channels of communication.

As you do practice layouts, record in your Tarot journal what Major Arcana cards appear, whether they are upright or reversed, what position they occupy, and how you interpret them in relationship to one another. This is especially important for beginners, who may become confused by cards that seem to be saying different things in the same spread.

A person's level of spiritual development influences the reading, too. Someone who is highly aware of and in touch with his own inner knowing, as well as with the higher realms, is likely to derive greater meaning from a reading than someone who has a more linear, materialistic worldview. If you genuinely wish to acquire wisdom, if you see the Tarot as teacher and vehicle for transferring insights, you'll undoubtedly be offered a great deal of information.

It is also possible that if you approach a reading with a pessimistic mindset, you are more likely to get a discouraging reading than if your outlook is optimistic. That's because the future isn't fixed. Outside forces don't dictate what happens; we create our own futures. If we expect a negative outcome, that's usually what we'll get. On the other hand, if we keep an open mind and hope for the best, we'll have a better chance of attracting good fortune.

## ASK CLEAR QUESTIONS

To get a lucid, meaningful response from the cards, you must be clear in your own mind and ask your question in a direct, unambiguous manner. One way to focus on your concern is to write the question on paper before you consult the Tarot. The physical act of writing your question pins it down and makes it more real. If you keep it in your head, you may allow other thoughts to intrude and convolute the original request.

Take a few minutes to think about what you really want to know. Relax, empty your head of all extraneous matters and distractions. Put all other considerations aside for the moment. Then write your question as concisely and precisely as possible. You can ask for a specific, straightforward, yes-or-no answer or simply request insight and guidance, depending on the situation and your intentions.

Let's say you are considering a job offer. If what you really want to know is, "Should I take the job I'm considering with XYZ company?" don't ask, "Is XYZ a good company to work for?" Even if XYZ is financially sound, highly respected, and fair to its employees, it still may not be the right place for you, or the particular position you've been offered might not be your best bet.

On a sheet of paper, write down exactly what you most want to know and the date, and then lay out the cards in the spread you've chosen. Record the spread on the paper, beneath the question, so you can keep a record of your query and refer back to it at a later date, if necessary. After getting an answer to your initial question, you can ask for additional information. If the cards have advised you to take the job, you now might ask, "What is the most important thing for me to be aware of in this new position?" or, "How can I best succeed in my new job?" or, "What will my relationships with coworkers and clients at XYZ be like?" If you simply seek general guidance, you could ask something like, "Please advise me about the job I'm considering with XYZ." If you have doubts or worries, address them, too. Again, write down each question and, underneath it, draw the spread you've laid to answer it. Continue asking related questions until you've received as much information as you desire.

Sometimes you may get an answer that seems incongruous or ambiguous. In such a case, you could try rephrasing the question. It's also possible that the situation you are asking about may contain conflicting or multilayered conditions. For instance, let's say you asked, "Will I be happy in the job I've been offered at XYZ?" and received a negative response, even though the cards had already advised you to accept the job. Perhaps other dynamics you can't understand at present may be in the works, so that both answers are true. Maybe you won't be happy in the job with XYZ but will make an important contact there that leads you to another job where you will be content.

---

It is human nature to be multifaceted; different strands of the person's life show up in the cards and open up issues for discussion. If, for example, The Hermit appears upright and The Devil appears also, it is an indication that the person needs to seek inner guidance (The Hermit) to resolve the problems or restrictions of The Devil.

---

The Tarot will usually respond to the most urgent matter on your mind or the one about which you feel most strongly—even if you ask something else. Therefore, if you are thinking about one thing and asking another, the reply might not make sense. Determine what's most important to you and write that down in the form of a question. From there you can make a list of additional questions, if you like, and work your way through the list in a logical, orderly fashion.

# UNDERSTAND THAT THE FUTURE IS NOT FIXED

Every decision and action you make influences what happens from here on. The future is not fixed. Each choice you make in life is equivalent to turning down a path at a crossroads; where you end up depends on the paths you've chosen in the past. Thus, the outcome signified by a Tarot reading is based on the conditions that exist at the time of the reading. If a situation changes, so will the outcome.

When you do a reading, for yourself or someone else, it's a good idea to stress the fact that the indicators shown in the reading are conditional; they describe what's likely to happen if things continue as they are going along now. If you continue to act and think and feel the same way as you do at the time of the reading, you'll experience the outcome that's shown. But if you change anything along the way, the outcome could change as well. Therefore, it's a good idea to update a reading every few months or so.

Many spreads address the past, present, and future—sometimes the near future and the distant future. Near future may mean a few days for one person and a few weeks for another, whereas distant future could indicate a few weeks to a few months, depending on the situation and the person for whom the reading is being done. As you become practiced at doing readings, you'll come to understand your own time frames.

It's probably useless to ask a question about what will happen ten years from now—many variables can influence the outcome between the present and that date. Many outcomes do, however, occur as predicted—even over long periods of time. That's because most of us tend to behave and think in predictable ways and to follow prescribed, comfortable, long-standing routines.

Some spiritual philosophies hold that everything is happening simultaneously—past, present, and future are illusions. "Now" and "future" are relative terms, and although the cards are good at showing what's likely to happen, they aren't quite so good at putting a time limit on it. Therefore, if you ask if something will occur within, say, a year, you may have to allow a little leeway.

# READING FOR YOURSELF

Reading for yourself is one of the best ways to learn the Tarot. When you do readings for other people, you may not be able to follow up after the reading. You won't always know if what you saw in the cards was valid or if your predictions came to pass. But when you read for yourself, you can check the information you get from the cards for accuracy and compare it with actual events.

Objectivity can be a problem when you are reading for yourself, though. It's easy to project your hopes or expectations onto the cards, or to ignore things you don't want to see. Standard interpretations, such as those presented in this and other introductory books on the Tarot, can help you balance your intuitive impressions and subjective responses with the impersonal, commonly-accepted views of other readers. You should study the ideas and opinions put forth by several different Tarot authors, rather than following only your own or only one teacher's interpretations. In time, you'll come to your own understanding, based on a blend of your experiences and observations, the work and writings of other Tarot readers, and your intuitive insights.

## THE SIGNIFICANCE OF A SIGNIFICATOR

Many Tarot spreads include a Significator, a card that represents you in the reading. The Significator acts as a link between the person for whom the reading is being done (yourself or someone else) and the other cards in the spread, which describe the circumstances of the reading. When you read for yourself, the Significator brings you into the reading; it serves as your representative for the duration of the reading.

Because the Court cards (King, Queen, Knight, and Page) depict people, they are popular choices for Significators. Often the Significator you choose relates to your sex, age, and astrological sign. For example, if you are a fire sign man over the age of thirty-five, who holds down an executive job or is active in the arts, and/or has light or reddish coloring, you would choose the King of Wands to represent you. If you are a sixteen-year-old Capricorn girl, you'd probably choose the Page of Pentacles as your Significator.

## ASTROLOGICAL SIGNIFICATORS

* **King of Wands:** A mature man, born under the zodiac sign Aries, Leo, or Sagittarius

* **Queen of Wands:** A mature woman, born under the zodiac sign Aries, Leo, or Sagittarius

* **Knight of Wands:** A young male, born under the zodiac sign Aries, Leo, or Sagittarius

* **Page of Wands:** A young female, born under the zodiac sign Aries, Leo, or Sagittarius

* **King of Pentacles:** A mature man, born under the zodiac sign Taurus, Virgo, or Capricorn

* **Queen of Pentacles:** A mature woman, born under the zodiac sign Taurus, Virgo, or Capricorn

* **Knight of Pentacles:** A young male, born under the zodiac sign Taurus, Virgo, or Capricorn

* **Page of Pentacles:** A young female, born under the zodiac sign Taurus, Virgo, or Capricorn

* **King of Swords:** A mature man, born under the zodiac sign Gemini, Libra, or Aquarius

* **Queen of Swords:** A mature woman, born under the zodiac sign Gemini, Libra, or Aquarius

* **Knight of Swords:** A young male, born under the zodiac sign Gemini, Libra, or Aquarius

* **Page of Swords:** A young female, born under the zodiac sign Gemini, Libra, or Aquarius

* **King of Cups:** A mature man, born under the zodiac sign Cancer, Scorpio, or Pisces

* **Queen of Cups:** A mature woman, born under the zodiac sign Cancer, Scorpio, or Pisces

* **Knight of Cups:** A young male, born under the zodiac sign Cancer, Scorpio, or Pisces

* **Page of Cups:** A young female, born under the zodiac sign Cancer, Scorpio, or Pisces

Keep in mind that you aren't limited to the Court cards. You may prefer to select a Major Arcana card, such as The Hermit, The Empress, or The Fool, to represent yourself. Or you might feel a connection to a card that depicts your state of mind at present—perhaps the artisan, shown by the Three of Pentacles, or the bored homemaker, depicted by the Four of Cups.

You can choose a Significator who will represent you in all readings, or you may decide to change Significators periodically, based on the circumstances surrounding the reading. If you've recently given up your corporate job to travel around the world, for example, you may decide the Knight of Wands now describes you better than the King of Pentacles. Another approach is to randomly draw a Significator from the pack before a reading—let your intuition determine who you are with respect to a particular reading.

## SETTING THE STAGE

Ideally, you'll want to designate a special place to study and read the cards. If you have an altar, a meditation area, or a separate room in your home that can be reserved for this purpose, so much the better, but any space you can make sacred will suffice. Some people like to enhance the space with candles, incense, flowers, crystals, icons, or artwork that holds meaning for them.

It is always a good idea to silently ask for divine guidance before using the Tarot cards. Some people like to meditate, pray, or engage in a ritual before doing a reading. When you feel calm and centered, begin shuffling your deck. Keep your mind open to receive information. Formulate your question and hold it in your mind while you handle the cards and write the question down if you wish.

## ONE-CARD READINGS

Ordinarily, unless you choose a fixed pattern of shuffling, there will come a point when it feels right to stop. At this point, place the entire deck in a single stack and cut three times, to the left, using your left hand. Then, restack the cards in the reverse order.

---

If one or more cards pop out of the deck while you are shuffling, consider them significant. You may choose to lay these cards to one side and view them as additional commentary on the reading to come. Or after considering them and how they apply to your query, insert them back into the deck and continue shuffling.

---

If you are totally unfamiliar with the Tarot deck, begin by doing a simple, one-card reading. After shuffling and cutting, you can either draw a card from the top of the deck or fan out the cards and select one at random. In your Tarot journal, note the date, your question or concern, and the card you drew. Study the card, first allowing images and impressions to present themselves to your imagination. Consider how these insights relate to your question. Then, look up the meaning of the card you selected and compare your initial impressions to the interpretation given in this or another book. Engage your intuition and use your imagination.

At first, your reactions to the individual cards may vary from seemingly nonsensical to extremely profound, or anything in between. No matter what your response is, write it down. Later on when you review your journal (as you should do periodically) new significance will be revealed.

Continue this one-card process until you have worked through all seventy-eight cards in the deck. This may take a while, as you are likely to repeatedly select certain cards that relate to the concerns, questions, and issues currently operating in your life. In time, you'll develop a good sense of each card's meaning and how it can be applied to a given situation. Review your journal or notebook frequently. Compare your interpretations of the same card on different dates to see if, and how, they have changed. Examine your interpretations of the same card in different circumstances. Were your impressions of the Eight of Cups different when your question involved a romantic relationship than when you asked about a family matter? Your personal experience with the cards through doing readings for yourself will serve as your primary source of information about their meanings.

Once you have acquired a working familiarity with all of the cards in the deck, you are ready to do more complicated readings. Now you can progress to laying out three, four, or five cards and start to see how the individual cards relate to each other to present a more complete picture.

⬦⬦⬦⬦⬦⬦⬦⬦⬦⬦⬦⬦⬦⬦⬦⬦⬦⬦⬦⬦⬦⬦⬦⬦⬦⬦⬦⬦⬦⬦⬦⬦⬦⬦⬦⬦⬦⬦⬦⬦⬦⬦⬦⬦⬦⬦⬦

If a card seems especially unrelated to your question, look at it several times during the day, recording any feelings it stirs in you. Before bed, review the card and your notes. If you have a dream that is influenced by the images on the card, record it also. Often, dreams comment on your daily readings.

⬦⬦⬦⬦⬦⬦⬦⬦⬦⬦⬦⬦⬦⬦⬦⬦⬦⬦⬦⬦⬦⬦⬦⬦⬦⬦⬦⬦⬦⬦⬦⬦⬦⬦⬦⬦⬦⬦⬦⬦⬦⬦⬦⬦⬦⬦⬦

# READING FOR OTHERS

When you are proficient at reading for yourself, you may wish to do Tarot readings for other people. Reading for others will expand your own understanding and present challenges you might not have encountered if you continued reading only for yourself. Different people bring different concerns and life experiences to the table, enabling you to see things in new and varied ways. A seventy-year-old woman, for example, will approach a reading in a different way than a twenty-year-old man. A homemaker with young children will have different concerns than a corporate executive. You can learn a great deal—about the Tarot and yourself—by reading for as many people as possible.

## BE CAREFUL WITH PREDICTIONS

If your primary reason for studying and using the Tarot is to do predictive readings for other people, be extremely careful about any pronouncements you make. Bear in mind always that many variables exist in the psychic world, that there is always a lot you don't know, even about your own psyche. Remember, too, that today's situation may well change in the future. Consequently, it's usually best to speak of trends and possibilities, rather than making absolute statements that apply to the future—especially when negative cards appear in a reading. You don't want to create a self-fulfilling prophecy by making a definite statement of future harm, ruin, disaster, or other ill fortune. It is much better to say something like, "It looks to me as if there might be a person around you who can't be trusted" or, "The indication is that you are experiencing anxiety and pain."

Let the person you are reading for give you feedback to confirm or deny your observations. If she or he can't relate to what you are saying, don't push it. The querent may not be able to hear or accept a negative interpretation, even if it is correct, and you have no way of knowing for certain that it is correct without the readee's validation. Always choose your words carefully when giving readings for others. You cannot know a person's inner state of mind, level of psychological savvy, or ability to receive information, especially if you are reading for strangers.

## BE CLEAR AND HONEST

When doing practice readings for others, it can be helpful to conduct a preliminary interview to determine what the querent hopes to achieve from the reading, so you can direct the reading accordingly.

Sometimes it happens that the surface question is a screen for what's really on the person's mind. In such cases, the Tarot will almost always speak to the real issue.

If you have friends who also read Tarot, you may enjoy reading for one another. This enables you to share insights and offer a variety of views and perspectives. Because each person's understanding is based on his or her experiences, a friend can provide information and ideas you might not have come up with on your own.

If you are in doubt about how to interpret a card or a spread, be honest and say something like, "It appears to me that such-and-such may happen, but I'm not quite sure I'm getting this clearly." Have no reluctance to admit that the information flow is murky, blocked, or unclear. Remember that you are practicing and learning. A reading is not a performance. Never assume that you know it all or that you can make absolute pronouncements.

It's also important to choose your words carefully and keep interpretations as clear and simple as possible. Avoid esoteric references and metaphysical explanations; do not confuse the issue with the use of technical terms that might be unfamiliar to your readee. Stick to plain English and offer your insights with the other person's needs in mind. What you and the cards communicate to a querent is only valid if it provides useful information or a new perspective.

## PREPARE YOURSELF EMOTIONALLY

Be prepared for emotional responses, even tears. Reading for others involves certain responsibilities, including giving aid and comfort. The people who come to you for advice often reveal private, sensitive matters, and you need to respect their privacy. They may be confused or in pain, and their vulnerability should be honored and treated with compassion. They place their trust in you, so you need to be totally honest, yet diplomatic.

Sometimes, of course, you may want to do readings just for fun—that is to say, on relatively trivial matters such as whether a friend should go on a blind date or how a vacation trip will turn out. Regardless of how weighty the concern, be sincere and considerate. Be prepared, however, that when minor questions are asked, more serious issues may lurk underneath, and those issues could be revealed by the Tarot cards.

# PRACTICE DIFFERENT SPREADS

In the beginning, it is always best to do practice readings for yourself until you have mastered the interpretations of the cards and developed your own slant on them. The best method for practicing readings is to choose a particular layout, preferably a simple one (such as the Four-Card spread), and use it each morning. Practice the same layout daily for two to four weeks or more, until it becomes second nature for you and you can easily put the pieces together to form a whole picture. Use the same layout to answer a variety of questions.

Once you have thoroughly familiarized yourself with a simple layout, pick a more complex one, such as the Celtic Cross spread or another spread you like. Practice it until you feel comfortable with it and understand all the different card positions, their significance in the reading, and how they relate to each other as a whole. Be consistent, working with one spread until you have mastered it.

As you work with the cards and notice the juxtapositions that occur, you will begin to understand how they all relate to one another, enriching the information flow and giving substance to the reading.

Continue in this manner until you have learned to use several different spreads that appeal to you. Some you'll like; others won't resonate with you. Some spreads are more appropriate to one type of question or situation than another. Do at least a few practice sessions with each spread just to find out how it sits with you. Which spreads to use is a matter of personal choice, but to choose wisely you need to have at least a working knowledge of many different ones. Later, you may enjoy creating your own spreads or developing your own variations on traditional spreads.

## HOW OFTEN SHOULD YOU DO READINGS?

You should do readings as often as you wish. In the beginning, when you are learning the meanings of the individual cards and studying the Tarot, it's a good idea to do one or more simple readings for yourself every day. As you become more adept, you may decide to do readings only when you need advice about a particular issue or situation.

You might wish to do regular readings about a situation that is ongoing or rapidly changing in your life, to get direction and guidance, or to see how things are evolving. However, if a matter is stable or not particularly pressing at this time, there's probably no point in doing a reading about it. You'll know when you need to do a reading. Something inside you will nudge you to pull out the cards.

Usually it's not wise to keep asking the same question, day after day, unless you really need guidance, something has changed, new information has come to light, or the matter is urgent. Doing so indicates doubt. Nor is it a good idea to ask the same question again if you didn't like the first answer you received. Doing so indicates you don't believe what the Tarot is telling you and don't respect your own inner knowing. Instead, ask for additional illumination or advice. Ask a different, but related question. Or wait a week or more before asking the question again.

# TAROT SPREADS

After you've learned the meanings of the individual cards, you can begin to combine them into significant patterns or spreads. Although we've already seen how a single Tarot card can answer a question and illuminate a situation, a grouping of several cards laid out in a prescribed pattern—what's known as a spread—will give you a great deal more information.

# ACQUAINTING YOURSELF WITH SPREADS

Spreads are configurations or arrangements of cards—usually three or more, and up to more than a dozen—designed to convey certain types of information. You could think of a spread as a puzzle that presents a picture when all the pieces are in place. The next chapter contains sixteen different spreads, some simple, some complex. In a spread, each position within the overall pattern means something specific. The relationships between the cards become as important as the individual cards themselves.

⬦⬦⬦⬦⬦⬦⬦⬦⬦⬦⬦⬦⬦⬦⬦⬦⬦⬦⬦⬦⬦⬦⬦⬦⬦⬦⬦⬦⬦⬦⬦⬦⬦⬦⬦⬦⬦⬦⬦⬦⬦⬦⬦⬦⬦⬦⬦⬦⬦⬦

By combining the meanings of the cards with the meanings of the positions in a spread, the insights provided are increased multiplicatively.

⬦⬦⬦⬦⬦⬦⬦⬦⬦⬦⬦⬦⬦⬦⬦⬦⬦⬦⬦⬦⬦⬦⬦⬦⬦⬦⬦⬦⬦⬦⬦⬦⬦⬦⬦⬦⬦⬦⬦⬦⬦⬦⬦⬦⬦⬦⬦⬦⬦⬦

No one knows where the old favorite spreads, such as the Celtic Cross, originated. Some spreads, such as the Tree of Life spread and the Feng Shui spread, are based on a particular spiritual or philosophical system. These layouts form designs that represent significant spiritual symbols, such as the Kabbalistic Tree of Life and the Chinese bagua, respectively. Other spreads are more open-ended and can be adapted to address a variety of possibilities. The cards in a three-card spread, for instance, may be viewed as signifying one of the following:

* The past, present, and future

* The physical, mental, and spiritual aspects of a question

* The situation, recommended action, and likely outcome

You'll probably find that some spreads appeal to you more than others or are more useful for your purposes. None is better than another; the choice of which spread(s) to use is yours entirely. After you become experienced at working with the Tarot, you might decide to design your own spreads or adapt traditional spreads to suit yourself.

# CHOOSING A SIGNIFICATOR

One of the first steps in laying out many spreads is to choose a Significator. A Significator is a card the querent selects to represent herself in a reading. This card usually is incorporated into the spread, although sometimes it is laid aside face up where it symbolizes the person for whom the reading is being done. In some cases, a Significator could represent a group or organization, a situation or event.

Choose a card that best describes the person or matter about which you are inquiring. You can either remove the Significator card from the pack or leave it in, according to the layout you are using. For instance, the Celtic Cross spread begins by the querent consciously picking a Significator, removing it from the deck, and placing it as the first card in the spread. Here, the Significator serves as the center, or grounding point, of the layout. If the Significator is left in the deck and it turns up in the spread, the position it occupies becomes particularly important.

If you like, you can use only the Major Arcana cards in a spread. In this case, your Significator will also be a trump card, and it plays a key role in your reading. Following are descriptions of the Major Arcana cards with suggestions for using them as Significators.

## THE FOOL

The Fool can stand for a child or young person, or for an innocent, naive individual who lacks experience in life. It can also be used to represent an adventure of any kind, such as when the reading involves a life change or a trip. Or The Fool can signify a decision that needs to be made, especially if the decision involves risk.

## THE MAGICIAN

The Magician can represent someone who has latent talent that he or she wants to bring to manifestation. This is a card of potential and describes a person with mental or magical power. Because its energy is masculine in expression, it can stand for a mature man who wields power of any kind. The Magician could represent someone in the field of applied sciences, such as engineering, medicine, or chemistry. He might also signify a man or woman with artistic ability who wants to put that talent to a practical use.

## THE HIGH PRIESTESS

As a Significator, The High Priestess represents secrets, intuition, and mystery. She could stand for a very private and mysterious person, or someone who is keeping a secret—or who wants to reveal a secret. It is a good Significator for anyone who is dedicated to the pursuit of knowledge, such as a scholar or researcher. Because The High Priestess represents a feminine archetype, this card can represent a mature female with psychic ability or a wise woman.

## THE EMPRESS

This card signifies a woman of substance, someone who is mature and capable at handling life's challenges. She occupies a position of authority, wealth, and power. She could be a politician, corporate executive, or someone aspiring to public office. The Empress can signify a creative person who is in command of her resources and expresses her talents productively, or someone with an earth mother personality. Also, she can represent a pregnant woman or one who has many children.

## THE EMPEROR

Use The Emperor to signify a man of authority, wealth, and power. A man in a profession that commands respect, such as the law or medicine, might also choose this card. The Emperor represents any male authority figure, such as a politician, a military officer, someone in law enforcement, a CEO of a corporation, or a government official.

## THE HIEROPHANT

This is the card of a teacher or mentor figure, especially someone who is in the clergy or member of an established institution, such as a university professor. The Hierophant can also represent a ceremonial figure with public duties, such as the head of an awards committee or grant-giving institution.

## THE LOVERS

This card can represent two people or a situation involving two people who have to cooperate with each other. This may mean a married or engaged couple, or a business partnership between two individuals. Issues concerning a love relationship, a friendship, or any one-on-one situation between two people could also be signified by The Lovers card.

## THE CHARIOT

This card can signify a messenger, or someone who is waiting to receive a message. A person who is involved in the transportation industry or the military service might also choose this Significator. Use The Chariot to represent any situation where conflicting elements are involved or need to be controlled, such as a group of people with different views or objectives.

## STRENGTH

Use this card to signify someone who is strong and in control—male or female. It can also symbolize a person with charisma and charm. Strength represents any situation where physical strength is required, such as athletics or exploration, or where inner strength and perseverance are factors.

## THE HERMIT

The Hermit is a good card to use if guidance is needed. He can symbolize someone who either seeks knowledge or possesses it—a wise man, professor, guru, or elder. The Hermit may be someone who prefers solitude to company, a recluse or monk, or a situation in which isolation is called for. A person who has retreated from ordinary life, or who desires to do so, might choose this card as a Significator. It can also signify anyone who is concerned about the past and delving into it, such as a researcher or historian.

## THE WHEEL OF FORTUNE

This card is not used to represent a person, but it can be chosen to signify a situation that has already been put into motion and is playing itself out.

## JUSTICE

Use this card to represent someone who is in the process of weighing a decision, or who is looking for information to help him/her make an important decision. Justice can also signify someone involved in the law, such as a judge, attorney, or arbitrator, or it may stand for the legal and jurisprudence system. Choose it as a Significator for someone who is involved in a lawsuit or other form of arbitration.

## THE HANGED MAN

This card represents a querent who is at a crossroads. It can be used to signify someone who is at a turning point in life or who feels he or she is at a standstill. The Hanged Man can also refer to someone who is in a hospital, or for whom an illness has provided the chance to embark on a new course.

## DEATH

Many people shy away from this card, and it is not usually chosen as a Significator. However, it is a good card to use when a situation involves a major transformation, such as the end of a relationship, the loss of a job, relocation, or any crisis that leads to a transformation.

## TEMPERANCE

Use this card as a Significator for a healer or caretaker—a nurse, doctor, psychotherapist, chiropractor, massage therapist, etc. Temperance can also be used to signify resourcefulness and conservation, or someone who manages resources wisely.

## THE DEVIL

This card can be used to signify someone who is depressed, engaged in obsessive/compulsive behavior, addicted to alcohol or drugs, or in a destructive state of mind. The Devil can also represent a person who feels trapped and can't see the way out. It refers to any restrictive situation that is limiting the querent's progress.

## THE TOWER

The Tower can be used as a Significator to depict an explosive situation or to represent the presence of forces beyond one's control. It is not generally used to signify a person.

## THE STAR

The Star can signify someone who is of a humanitarian bent, offering aid to others without expectation of recompense or reward. It can also stand for a person who entertains others, such as an actor or musician, or someone who is an inspired artist. A beautiful person of either sex could be indicated by The Star, as well.

## THE MOON

The Moon can be used to represent someone who is moony, or loony. There are many associations with the moon in life—the maiden or virgin, the mother, the wise woman—and this card could depict any of them. The Moon is linked with Artemis, the "Lady of the Beasts," and all in nature that is wild and free. Use The Moon card to signify anyone who strongly relates to the inner feminine.

### THE SUN

The Sun card is the usual Significator for children, or situations concerning children. It can also be used when you want to throw light onto a situation, or to bring something into the light of day. Someone with a sunny, radiant personality might also choose this card as a Significator.

### JUDGMENT

Use this card when the querent is either in the process of becoming more aware of what he needs to do, or who should be developing this awareness. Judgment represents someone who is seeking the truth about a particular situation or who must make a clear judgment in a situation.

### THE WORLD

This card represents a self-actualized and fulfilled person. It can also signify a situation that is going especially well. Use it as a Significator for someone who is involved in the natural sciences or environmental work.

## LAY OUT THE SPREAD

If a Significator is called for, select it from the deck. Then choose a spread you feel is suitable to the question or issue at hand and lay out the cards according to the instructions in the next chapter. Different spreads are designed to answer different sorts of questions or to comment on certain types of situations. If you don't know which spread is best for your question, you can use the Celtic Cross spread. This versatile pattern was recommended by Arthur Edward Waite as "the most suitable for obtaining an answer to a definite question."

Next, proceed with whatever shuffling method you have decided to use. Many readers encourage the querent to shuffle the cards, to put his or her vibrations on them. Other readers prefer not to let anyone else touch their cards. The choice is up to you. No matter how you shuffle, or who shuffles, the cards will automatically arrange themselves as they should be. Count on it! The order in which they come up is never an accident.

The querent (you or someone else) then cuts the cards. After cutting and reassembling the deck, begin dealing the spread from the top of the deck. Some readers lay the cards face down; others, face up. Again, the choice is yours. Regardless of whether the querent sits across from or beside the reader, the cards are always read as they face the reader. If you deal cards face down, be sure to turn them up from left to right so that you don't reverse upright cards or turn reversed cards upright.

Reading Tarot is like playing a piece of classical music. The score is written by the original composer, but every performer plays the music slightly differently, according to his or her own individual interpretation.

Some writers on the Tarot insist that the rest of the deck be kept face down at all times. Once a layout is dealt, the remaining cards may be laid aside and left out of the reading. Or if you prefer, hold the unused part of the deck as you read and, when it seems appropriate, for elucidation or to answer further questions regarding the matter, draw cards at random from the deck. As you continue doing readings, you will develop your own methods. There is no right way.

# INTERPRET THE SPREAD

It's important to look at any spread first as a whole. Before you start interpreting the individual cards and their placements, look at the overall picture. What colors are most evident? Are the images powerful and dramatic or peaceful and benign? Is the general tone one of contrasts or of harmony? How do you feel when you gaze at the spread?

Next, check for similarities, voids, preponderances, or weaknesses. Does the spread contain many Major Arcana cards or mostly Minor Arcana ones? Are Court cards present? Aces? Are there many cards from the same suit? Is any suit absent? Do several of the numbered cards bear the same number?

## TIMELINES AND LEVELS OF AWARENESS

If the spread indicates a timeline, as is the case with the Past-Present-Future spread and the Celtic Cross, notice which cards appear in the beginning and at the end of the time period represented. If the "past" includes negative cards and the "future" shows positive ones, you can see definite progress being made and better days ahead. If the opposite is evident, it could indicate that you aren't handling the situation appropriately or that things may get worse before they get better.

If the spread is designed to describe various levels of awareness, such as the World Tree spread, note whether the different levels are harmonious or incongruous. Are the images shown in one section calm, the others disturbing? Or do they seem to flow together in a coordinated manner? In a spread such as the Horoscope spread or the Feng Shui spread, which describe different areas of your life, check to see if positive cards turn up in some areas while negative ones appear in others. Do the cards fall into positions that seem to correspond to or conflict with their basic natures?

## NUMBERS IN SPREADS

Pay attention to the numbers shown on the pip cards and where they fall in the spread. Do you see lots of Fours and Eights, indicating stability, or Fives suggesting change? In a time-oriented spread, do low numbers turn up early in the spread and higher numbers later on? This can show development with regard to the subject of the reading. Consider the numbers on the trump cards as well as those on the Minor Arcana cards.

After you've assessed the spread from a broad perspective, you can zero in on the meanings of the individual cards in their respective positions. By combining the meanings of each card with its position, you can gain highly personal and detailed information.

## WHICH SPREAD SHOULD YOU USE?

Which spread to use depends on the nature of your question and what you want to know. Let's say you've recently met a man who interests you, and you are curious about the possibilities of a relationship with him. If you simply want to know whether you should consider him as a prospective partner, you could use one of the Yes/No methods. Or you could try the Single-Card technique (explained in the next chapter), which will give you some clues to the man's character. Or pick a single card from the deck. A positive card suggests pursuing things further; a negative card says don't waste your time.

❖❖❖❖❖❖❖❖❖❖❖❖❖❖❖❖❖❖❖❖❖❖❖❖❖❖❖❖❖❖❖❖❖❖❖❖❖❖❖❖❖❖❖❖❖❖

You can do the Horoscope spread on your birthday to gain an overview of the coming year, but it can also be useful if you want to see how a particular decision or matter will affect your entire life.

❖❖❖❖❖❖❖❖❖❖❖❖❖❖❖❖❖❖❖❖❖❖❖❖❖❖❖❖❖❖❖❖❖❖❖❖❖❖❖❖❖❖❖❖❖❖

If your initial indicators are good, and you'd like to know how to proceed with this man, you could use the Four-Card spread. This describes the situation, an obstacle or opportunity you may encounter, what action you should take, and the likely outcome to the relationship. The Immediate Situation Three-Card spread could be useful, too.

Once you've entered into a relationship with this man, you might feel a need to get more advice or information about him and your situation. The Horseshoe spread or the Practical Advice Five-Card spread can reveal some of the hidden influences at work and recommend how to address them. After you've been together a while, you might choose the Thirteen-Card Story spread, which explains the progression of the relationship and provides insight into the situations that have occurred between you.

Although the simpler spreads can be used on a regular or even daily basis, the more involved ones, such as the Tree of Life spread and the Feng Shui spread, deal with larger areas of life and longer periods of time. It's probably best to use these only once or twice a year, unless a significant change has occurred.

# THE SIGNIFICANCE OF TRUMPS IN A SPREAD

Major Arcana cards represent spiritual or universal forces, higher consciousness, the collective, and archetypes. When they turn up in a spread, they could be considered messages from the Divine. This may indicate that you are being helped or influenced by powers beyond your own immediate everyday awareness, or that aspects of the reading (or the subject of the reading) have implications beyond the obvious, physical ones—even beyond your own personal existence. A spread with many trumps in it shows that the matter is complex and involves different levels of being. It can suggest that to handle the issue, you need to ask for assistance from a higher power and trust that power to guide you.

Some people view the trumps as indicators that fate or destiny is operating with regard to the subject of the reading. To other readers, the presence of Major Arcana cards means you are seeing the results of past actions starting to manifest in your life.

## TRUMP POSITION

Notice the positions of the Major Arcana cards. Do they appear in the early or past portion of a spread or toward the end or future part? Do they represent opportunities or obstacles? Do they show areas you are aware of or hidden influences? Whenever a trump card turns up in a spread, pay extra attention to it, for it can reveal a great deal.

You will notice as you do readings that shuffling the cards can cause some of them to get turned upside down. When cards appear upside down in a spread, they are said to be reversed. Some readers simply turn reversed cards upright again. Others interpret cards differently when they are reversed than when they are upright.

## IMPORTANCE OF REVERSED CARDS

Much disagreement exists concerning the significance of reversed cards. Many Tarot readers consider a reversed card to be weakened, so that it has less impact than it would if it were upright. Another popular view suggests that reversed cards depict more negative, dark, or malevolent energies at work. In her book *Tarot Reversals*, Mary K. Greer offers an interesting opinion: "Reversals reveal the esoteric or hidden components, the shamanic perspective of the world, and a place known as the dream-time or inner planes versus so-called 'reality.'" Reversals encourage us to see beyond and through the obvious, and to consider a matter's underlying dynamics as well as its apparent ones.

Whether you choose to interpret reversed cards in a spread or read only upright positions is up to you. You may wish to work with the Tarot for a while before you decide whether to interpret reversals in a different manner, and if so, how.

# CREATING YOUR OWN SPREADS

After you know what the cards mean and have experimented with a number of different layouts, you can feel free to design your own spreads. A spread is like a blueprint of the reading you are going to do; through its pattern, you build the reading. You can include as many or as few cards as you like in a spread. You can expand on standard layouts, or you can design a completely original layout pattern. You are limited only by your imagination.

Begin by identifying exactly what it is you want to know and what you want the spread to convey. Then organize those issues into an ordered plan, marking each card's position according to what it will signify. By doing this, you are telling your unconscious that you want specific answers to your questions, and you are determining the method you will use to access the information you seek.

Let's say a person has had an auto accident and thinks there is some deeper reason than bad driving for what's happened. This individual wants to explore that issue in depth by consulting the Tarot. By having a dialogue with the readee, you go through a process of clarification by asking questions, such as "What role is this accident playing in my life now?"; "How did I participate in this accident?"; "What purpose are the accident and its results serving in my life?"; "Why did I have this accident?"; "What am I getting out of having had this accident?"; "Am I avoiding something by having had an accident?"; and so forth.

---

As an example of an expansion of a pre-existing layout, the three-card spread can be expanded into a nine-card spread by using three layers of three cards each and designating each layer as past, present, or future.

---

You then organize the questions into a card plan. Draw your layout and designate a card position that corresponds to each question. Number the card positions on the plan. You decide how many cards to use, depending on how many questions or facets of the issue you wish to have answered. Then choose a layout pattern that appeals to both you and the person for whom the reading is being done. The visual pattern of the spread can be varied according to your personal inclinations: Some people work best with linear shapes, others with circular patterns, and still others with rectangles or star shapes. You can combine both your concept and your aesthetic sense in the layout, for this invites your intuition to speak through it.

As you order the questions and place the card positions in the plan, you may decide to drop some questions and add others. Include the readee in the entire process. You might, for example, want to add to the previous list such questions as, "What are the past influences that led to the accident?" and/or, "How will this accident affect my future?"

You can also design multipurpose spreads that can be used to address a wide range of issues and questions. Base them on your personal belief system or a special interest, if you like.

# SIXTEEN SPREADS

Spreads are configurations of Tarot cards that have been designed to convey information in a particular way. The simplest spreads use only a single card; complex patterns may involve more than a dozen. A reading can include one or several spreads, depending on the situation and what you want to know. The sixteen spreads here offer a variety of approaches. You should experiment with all of them to see which ones work best for you. Each explanation is followed by an example to help you understand when and how to use each spread.

# SINGLE-CARD METHOD

This is the easiest and most basic of all spreads, and it can be used to answer all types of questions. Although you won't get as much in-depth information as you would from a longer, more complex spread, this method can be surprisingly helpful—especially in answering straight-forward questions for which you need an immediate answer.

Shuffle and cut the cards while thinking about your question. Then draw a single card from the pack. You can either pick the top card from the deck or fan out all the cards face down and select one at random.

### AN EXAMPLE OF THE SINGLE-CARD METHOD

Ellen felt that a friend was angry with her, but when she asked what was wrong her friend said, "Nothing's wrong." Ellen turned to the Tarot and asked for insight into the tension she experienced between herself and her friend. She drew the Four of Swords, which she interpreted as an indication that her friend was tired and needed some time alone to rest and relax. As it turned out, the friend had been under a lot of stress at work, and the pressure was causing her to behave in a brusque, impatient way, even though she wasn't really angry at Ellen.

# YES/NO METHOD

To use the Yes/No method, you need only decide which cards will represent Yes and which No. After the usual shuffling and cutting, draw a single card from the deck, either from the top or at random. Consider the card's meaning, too, for this will provide further information. You may use the following guidelines for determining which cards signify Yes and which ones signify No or you may opt to create a system of your own. There are no firm rules, but here are some guidelines:

### *Major Arcana*

* If you are willing to work with the concept of the card: Yes

* If you are unwilling to do the work: No

### Minor Arcana

* Even Numbers: Yes
* Odd Numbers: No

### Court Cards

* King: No
* Queen: Yes
* Knight: No
* Page: Yes

Once you have decided which cards mean Yes and which indicate No, you should also consider whether your chosen card is upright or reversed.

### Upright

If it's a Yes card, the upright position represents a definite Yes.
If it's a No card, the upright position indicates a definite No.

### Reversed

If Yes, there will be a delay.
If No, there will be obstacles to prevent you.

## AN EXAMPLE OF THE YES/NO METHOD

John was thinking of buying a house in the country and unexpectedly found exactly what he was looking for, but the price was higher than he wanted to pay. However, someone else had put a bid in, and he had to make an immediate decision. He opted for a Yes/No reading—should he buy the house? The card that came up was the Ten of Pentacles, upright—a definite Yes. Since the Ten of Pentacles signifies acquisition of a home and success in money matters, John was being advised to buy the house in confidence, that he would have the financial wherewithal. The card also indicated it was the right choice and that he would be happy there.

# EITHER/OR METHOD

Use this spread when you have two options and can't decide between them. After shuffling and cutting the deck, select two cards either from the top or at random from the pack. The first card represents one option; the second card signifies the other choice.

## AN EXAMPLE OF THE EITHER/OR METHOD

Jennifer had two job offers. To determine which she should accept, she used the Either/Or method. To represent the smaller and less well-known of the two companies, she drew the Queen of Swords, which suggested that they would respect her as an employee and treat her well. Her work was likely to be well-publicized if she contracted with them and she could gain recognition. Jennifer drew the Four of Pentacles to stand for the larger, more established company. This card indicated that although she would receive a larger amount of money from this company, she couldn't expect as much potential growth, fame, or satisfaction if she accepted their offer.

# PAST-PRESENT-FUTURE METHOD

This three-card spread lets you see the past influences or conditions regarding a situation, the present state of the matter, and what's likely to occur in the future. After shuffling and cutting the deck, select three cards either from the top of the pack or at random. Lay them out side by side. The card on the left represents the past; the middle card shows the present; the card on the right indicates the future.

## AN EXAMPLE OF THE PAST-PRESENT-FUTURE METHOD

Tom had reconnected with an old girlfriend after many years and wondered what their chances were now for a happy relationship. He shuffled and cut the cards, then dealt three from the top of the deck.

The past card was The Fool, which suggested he'd been too young when the couple first met and had not been ready for a serious commitment. The Six of Cups turned up in the present spot, showing renewed affection. In the future position, Tom laid the Seven of Cups, an indication that many possibilities existed and that his own attitude would play an important role in the outcome.

# IMMEDIATE SITUATION THREE-CARD SPREAD

This simple, quick layout focuses on what's happening now and provides insight into the matter at hand. It's a good spread to use when you want to focus on a particular situation, clarify what's happening, and receive insight or a new perspective.

**Card 1:** *The nature of the present situation*
**Card 2:** *Your attitude toward what's happening*
**Card 3:** *The key element for you to consider*

## AN EXAMPLE OF AN IMMEDIATE SITUATION THREE-CARD SPREAD

Imagine the following results for a reading for Irene, a married woman with two young children, who requested a reading because she suspected her husband wanted a divorce, even though he did not actually say so.

### Card 1: The Chariot

In the position of the nature of the present situation, The Chariot indicated that Irene needed to stay centered and not get overly emotional about her suspicions, which were unproven. She had to steer a middle course between her conflicting thoughts and emotions and get them both moving forward in tandem, instead of pulling her in opposite directions.

### Card 2: Three of Swords

The Three of Swords in the attitude position indicated that Irene had already made up her mind that she and her husband were going to separate. She was depressed and angry and in pain but felt no hope for mending the situation.

### Card 3: The Empress

The Empress card in the key position advised her to be mindful of herself as a mother as well as a wife. She needed to address issues of communication with her husband, which were at the root of the problem. The Empress told Irene to be more loving and nurturing and less critical of what she considered his shortcomings. She had Venus in Virgo, which indicated her tendency to criticize her partner. The Empress is related to Venus, which rules marriage, a sign that the marriage would survive if she shared her feelings and learned to give and receive love uncritically.

## FOUR-CARD SPREAD

This spread offers advice for dealing with a specific concern. Its strength is its simple, direct approach to dealing with practical, everyday problems. Shuffle and cut the cards, then lay them out side by side in a horizontal line, from left to right.

**Card 1:** *Situation*

**Card 2:** *Obstacle*

**Card 3:** *Action recommended*

**Card 4:** *Outcome*

# AN EXAMPLE OF THE FOUR-CARD SPREAD

Mark had held his present job for nearly three years. Despite his abilities and efforts, he had been overlooked for several promotions and wondered why he couldn't seem to get ahead.

## Card 1: Four of Cups

This card described Mark's present situation. He was bored and felt stuck in a rut. He no longer had any enthusiasm for his job, but he couldn't muster the courage to make a change.

## Card 2: The Devil

As the obstacle card, The Devil suggested that Mark's own fear and doubt, as well as his excessive concern with security, were blocking his progress. Even though he was a reliable and hard-working employee, he lacked self-confidence. As a result, his employers were reluctant to promote him to a position of greater authority and responsibility.

## Card 3: Knight of Wands

Knights often represent movement, and in Mark's case, laying this card in the action spot advised him to seek another job with another company where he'd have more opportunity for advancement. This card also recommended that Mark be more adventurous and willing to take the risk involved in changing jobs.

## Card 4: Ace of Pentacles

As an outcome card, an Ace indicates the likelihood of a new beginning—in this case, one that involves money or material resources (pentacles). Thus the reading strongly shows that Mark would benefit from finding a new job.

# PRACTICAL ADVICE FIVE-CARD SPREAD

As the name suggests, this simple spread is good for gaining insight into practical matters. After shuffling and cutting, lay the cards out from left to right in a single row.

**Card 1:** *Past influence*

**Card 2:** *Present influence*

**Card 3:** *Major influence*

**Card 4:** *Advice*

**Card 5:** *Outcome likely if advice is followed*

## AN EXAMPLE OF A PRACTICAL ADVICE FIVE-CARD SPREAD

The querent was Joshua, a young man only a year away from graduating college. He was considering taking off a year after graduation before going to work and wanted advice.

### Card 1: Ten of Wands

This card in the position of past influence indicated that Joshua had been shouldering a heavy load for a long time, working a part-time job in addition to carrying a full load of course work.

### Card 2: Two of Pentacles

This card in the position of present influence revealed that Joshua was receiving money from more than one source. His parents helped out, and he had a student loan as well as his part-time job. It further indicated that he was constantly juggling money matters, which put both external and internal pressure on him to join the workforce immediately after graduation.

### Card 3: Four of Swords

This card appearing in the major influence spot indicated that Joshua was overtired and badly needed a rest. He needed time for respite and meditation, to be alone and get in touch with his inner self instead of being pushed about by outside circumstances and the expectations of others.

### Card 4: The Fool

The appearance of The Fool in the advice position recommended that Joshua should have the experience of freedom and enjoy his youth, at least for a while, before buttoning himself up in the corporate world. This card advised him to go out and experience the world as a free spirit, to put aside his fears and worries about making the right career moves as soon as he graduated. He was being advised by The Fool to have faith, to take a leap into his unknown future, to go adventuring with a carefree attitude before settling down to the serious business of a lifetime of working.

### Card 5: The World

The World card in the position of the likely outcome, if he follows The Fool's advice, is that he will travel and see the world. In the end all will be well, and success will be his. In other words, the world's his oyster if he goes willingly where The Fool leads.

# TRADITIONAL CELTIC CROSS SPREAD

This popular and versatile spread calls for a Significator. Place it on the table to bring you (or the person for whom the reading is being done) into the reading and lay Card 1 on top of the Significator.

*Card 1:* *This covers you and describes your immediate concerns.*

*Card 2:* *This crosses you and describes obstacles facing you.*

*Card 3:* *This crowns you and describes what is known to you objectively.*

*Card 4:* *This is beneath you and describes the foundation of the concern or past influences affecting the situation. It can also show what is unknown about the situation.*

*Card 5:* *This is behind you and describes past influences now fading away.*

*Card 6:* *This is before you and describes new circumstances coming into being—the near future.*

*Card 7:* *This is your self and describes your current state of mind.*

*Card 8:* *This is your house and describes the circumstances surrounding the situation.*

*Card 9:* *This is what you hope or fear, perhaps what you both want and fear.*

*Card 10:* *This is what will come and describes the likely future outcome.*

# AN EXAMPLE OF A CELTIC CROSS READING

The querent was Sue, a middle-aged woman with a Pisces sun sign and an emotional nature, so the reader chose the Queen of Cups as her Significator.

## Card 1: Seven of Pentacles

She was concerned about money because she had lost her job due to ill health and was totally dependent on her husband for financial support.

## Card 2: King of Pentacles

Sue's husband was well-off and owned his own business, but he was a dominating man who held on to money tightly. Naturally timid, Sue was afraid of him. His obvious masculine power and the financial advantage he held over her made her feel powerless in his presence.

## Card 3: The Moon

Her unconscious creative forces were suggesting she could, despite her ill health, work to develop her artistic creativity, which she had all but squelched. In astrology, the moon represents the public, so this card showed that she might eventually make money with her talent.

## Card 4: Justice

Sue was involved in a class-action lawsuit regarding her illness. She was hoping for a hefty financial settlement, which would free her from dependence on her husband, whom she wished to divorce.

## Card 5: Nine of Swords

This card suggested that Sue's pain and travail were coming to an end, and that a solution to her emotional problems and financial worries would be found.

## Card 6: The Wheel of Fortune

This card indicated that forces she had already put into motion—the lawsuit—were continuing and that there would be a favorable result that would allow her to make significant changes in her life.

### Card 7: Strength

This card clearly indicated that underneath her seeming passivity and timidity Sue had inner strength that would see her through this difficult time.

### Card 8: Knight of Cups

This card showed Sue was receiving loving support from her son who had recently suggested she leave her husband (his stepfather) and move to another state to live with him and his wife.

### Card 9: The Chariot, reversed

The Chariot reversed indicates that Sue was afraid of losing control over her life and that her lack of self-confidence had stopped her from extricating herself from her unhappy marriage.

### Card 10: Nine of Pentacles

This card shows that Sue will become financially independent, probably through the success of the lawsuit, and be able to live alone.

## GENERAL LIFE CONDITIONS SPREAD

This spread can be used to answer just about any question. It provides insight into the querent's psychological state while shedding light on practical matters.

*Card 1:* Who you are right now
*Card 2:* What is affecting you
*Card 3:* What you value
*Card 4:* What's bothering you
*Card 5:* The short term
*Card 6:* The long term

# AN EXAMPLE OF A GENERAL LIFE CONDITIONS SPREAD

The querent was Janice, a married woman with a learning-disabled child and an unemployed husband.

### Card 1: Ten of Wands

The Ten of Wands in the "Who are you?" position said that Janice was carrying a full burden of responsibility on her shoulders, but that she was managing the situation successfully and working hard.

### Card 2: Five of Pentacles

The Five of Pentacles in the "What's affecting you?" position indicated money difficulties as a major concern. Due to her husband's unemployment, Janice was the only earner and had applied to receive food stamps.

### Card 3: The Hierophant

In the "What do you value?" position, The Hierophant indicated that her deeply felt religious belief was the glue holding Janice together during this time of trial and difficulty.

### Card 4: Two of Pentacles

In the position of what is bothering her, we find the Two of Pentacles, indicating that she had been juggling finances to make ends meet since her husband had been out of work. Still, it is a positive card that could indicate extra income, perhaps from part-time work.

### Card 5: Ace of Pentacles

In the position of the short term, the Ace of Pentacles said that new money was on its way to Janice and would arrive soon. She had a settlement pending as a result of an accident, and this Ace indicated it would be adjudicated quickly, and that the money received would ease her situation.

### Card 6: Ten of Cups

In the long-term position, the Ten of Cups was a strong indication that Janice's family would soon be moving into a new positive cycle of emotional well-being and happiness in family matters.

# QUICK ANSWER SPREAD

After shuffling and cutting the deck, lay out the cards in a horizontal row, from left to right.

**Card 1:** *Concern*

**Card 2:** *Immediate past*

**Card 3:** *Immediate future*

**Card 4:** *Querent's state of mind*

**Card 5:** *Obstacle*

**Card 6:** *Help*

**Card 7:** *Outcome*

## AN EXAMPLE OF A QUICK ANSWER SPREAD

Debra was a single woman in her late twenties who had always lived with her parents. She wanted to get out on her own and live in a warm climate and was thinking of moving from New York to Florida.

### Card 1: Four of Wands

This card in the concern position indicated that leaving her family and the happiness and security it had always provided for her was a major issue. Being on her own for the first time, she knew she would miss her close-knit family life.

### Card 2: Queen of Pentacles, reversed

This card represented Debra's mother, who had always indulged her daughter with material things but was a domineering, controlling woman. She was angry that her daughter wanted to move away and they had recently quarreled bitterly about it.

### Card 3: Eight of Wands

This card in the immediate future suggested that Debra would take a trip, probably soon and by air. The cards indicated that she should take her vacation in Florida. She could check out the job market and see how she felt about making her home there.

### Card 4: Five of Pentacles

This card showed that uppermost in her mind was her fear of living on her own. She worried that she would not be able to make it financially, which her mother had brought up during their quarrel.

### Card 5: The Fool, reversed

This card in the obstacle position indicated that Debra was afraid to take chances. She feared risking making a fool of herself by not being able to manage on her own, having to return home, and admitting failure.

### Card 6: Ace of Pentacles

This card appearing in the help position suggested that new money and opportunities for making money were coming to her, and that her fears of poverty were unfounded.

### Card 7: The Sun

The Sun card in the outcome position was an indication that she would be successful—in a sunny climate! The move to Florida would free her from the oppressive sense of guilt and obligation she felt to her parents for their support. The Sun card clearly said, "Go for it; I'm with you!"

# THE HORSESHOE SPREAD

Each card position in this spread represents a specific area of life. After shuffling and cutting the deck, lay out the cards from right to left. There is also a ten-card version of the Horseshoe spread, but the seven-card layout is a bit simpler.

***Card 1:*** *The past. Describes what past events, emotions, and actions pertain to the question being asked.*

***Card 2:*** *The present. Refers to what's happening now or the querent's current state of mind regarding what has just occurred.*

***Card 3:*** *Hidden influences. This position indicates unexpected influences, occurrences, or expectations about which the querent is unaware.*

***Card 4:*** *Obstacles. Describes what is standing in the querent's way of attaining her desires. The obstacles may be outer conditions or problems in the querent's attitude.*

***Card 5:*** *The environment. Describes other people, or another person, and their attitudes toward the querent and her issue.*

***Card 6:*** *What should be done. This position shows action to be taken or recommends a change in attitude.*

***Card 7:*** *The most likely outcome. What's likely to occur, assuming you follow the advice given by Card 6.*

## AN EXAMPLE OF A HORSESHOE SPREAD

The querent was Kim, a young woman who wanted to know if the romantic relationship in which she was involved would develop into marriage.

### Card 1: Three of Swords

This card indicated that the relationship had already been plagued by separation. The on-again, off-again affair had caused Kim much pain and anxiety.

### Card 2: Knight of Cups

This card revealed that Kim had recently had a communication from him indicating he wanted to get back together, suggesting he might be ready for commitment.

### Card 3: The Empress, reversed

This card warned that Kim was thinking of accidentally getting pregnant to force a marriage, a course of action that would doom her to failure.

### Card 4: Queen of Pentacles

This card represented Kim's mother, who strongly opposed her daughter's choice. Her family was well-off and socially well-connected; the young man was from a blue-collar background and was working his way through college.

### Card 5: Strength

The appearance of this card indicated Kim was ready to declare her independence and marry her lover.

### Card 6: Temperance

This card counseled patience and self-control. It cautioned Kim not to rush into anything but to work to reconcile the opposing forces, to allow her mother to realize the young man's good qualities, and to have the maturity to accept that things often take time.

### Card 7: Ten of Cups

This card indicates that if Kim follows the advice given and does not use any trickery or deceit to get her man, the result will be a happy marriage blessed with children and prosperity.

# THE WORLD TREE SPREAD

This pattern is based on the Celtic pagan concept of a World Tree, a sacred oak that connects the three realms of existence. The roots reach into the underworld, which is not the same as the Christian hell, but rather is the primal source from which life emerges. The trunk crosses through the earthly realm as we know it, and the branches stretch into the heavens or realm of the spirit. Use this spread when you want to understand the relationship between the three layers of reality or the three levels of the querent's consciousness.

*Cards 1, 2, and 3:* *Influences in the subconscious or underworld. These three root cards describe the source or roots of the situation. They may exist in the querent's subconscious, or they may be hidden spiritual forces, perhaps conditions stemming from past lifetimes.*

*Cards 4 and 5:* *The present situation. The two trunk cards show physical or conscious conditions, and they may also indicate how the querent is working with the forces described by the root cards.*

*Cards 6, 7, 8, 9, and 10:* *Influences in the spiritual realm or higher self. The cards that make up the branches represent spiritual forces and the querent's higher consciousness.*

# AN EXAMPLE OF THE WORLD TREE SPREAD

The querent was Alice, a woman artist in her thirties whose parents were alcoholics. Through her personal growth work and spiritual studies, she was attempting to release the fear and anger stemming from her childhood and to develop more faith and self-confidence.

### Cards 1, 2, and 3: The Devil, Five of Pentacles, Nine of Swords

The Devil in this position reveals the deep-seated doubt, rage, and self-loathing Alice was holding onto, destructive emotions that had a crippling effect on her. The Five of Pentacles told of the poverty in which she'd grown up, as well as the insecurity that still plagued her in adulthood. The Nine of Swords showed that Alice's fears and disappointments, although based on real conditions in the past, were now only memories that she was allowing to continue causing her pain.

### Cards 4 and 5: The High Priestess, Three of Cups

The High Priestess shows that Alice was very intuitive and imaginative and was using these qualities in the present to try to heal the suffering from her childhood. At present, she is working on a series of paintings that express the difficulties in her youth and her growth through her current Buddhist spiritual practice, which is helping her to release the past. The Three of Cups represents a group of fellow artists whose encouragement and friendship bring Alice much happiness and whom she views as her new family.

### Cards 6, 7, 8, 9, and 10: Queen of Wands, Three of Pentacles, Six of Cups, Strength, Nine of Pentacles

These cards show the guidance and help that Alice's higher self offers and the spiritual forces that are present in her life. The Queen of Wands shows the creative talent she possesses. The Three of Pentacles represents benefits from putting her abilities to use. The Six of Cups suggests renewed love and joy in her life, as a result of her group of artist friends and her spiritual path. Strength says that Alice has powerful protective forces operating at a spiritual level, and that she is inwardly much stronger than she believes herself to be. The Nine of Pentacles also points out that she is capable of making her own way and reaping the rewards, self-confidence, and security she desires.

## THE TREE OF LIFE SPREAD

Based on the Kabbalistic Tree of Life, this spread provides insights into the querent's spiritual nature as well as the outer conditions that are related to the matter at hand. The card positions correspond to the ten sephirot (which represent the ten characteristics of divinity) on the tree. (Note: The Tree of Life spread is read from the bottom up, from Card 10 to Card 1.)

**Card 1:** *Light*
*(outcome)*

**Card 2:** *Wisdom*
*(goals, changes, power)*

**Card 3:** *Understanding*
*(receptivity, creativity, limitations)*

**Card 4:** *Mercy*
*(abundance, generosity, memories)*

**Card 5:** *Severity, strength*
*(struggle, activity, destruction)*

**Card 6:** *Beauty*
*(love, compassion, new insights)*

**Card 7:** *Victory*
*(romance, emotions, desires)*

**Card 8:** *Glory*
*(knowledge, analysis, discrimination)*

**Card 9:** *Foundation*
*(sexual issues, illusions, fears, the unconscious)*

**Card 10:** *Kingdom*
*(physicality, money, practical matters)*

# AN EXAMPLE OF A TREE OF LIFE SPREAD

The querent was Kyle, a man of thirty with musical talent and ambitions. He wanted to quit his "day job" to devote himself to developing his talent and wondered if this was the right choice.

### Card 10: Eight of Pentacles

This card in the money and practicality position signified that Kyle would be learning new skills, becoming an apprentice at a new trade or career. It augured well for his being able to make money with his music, especially considering that he was full of enthusiasm and determination and practical enough to manage his limited funds until his new career took off.

### Card 9: Queen of Wands, reversed

This card represented Kyle's wife, a beautiful and ambitious woman who was against him risking their financial security. He wanted her support but feared her disapproval and worried that if he didn't make enough money she might leave him despite their strong sexual attraction to each other.

### Card 8: Three of Pentacles

This is the card of the craftsman, which indicated Kyle had the knowledge needed to practice his art and will keep developing his abilities in a discriminating way. It also suggests that he will make money with his creative talents, for he is good at what he does. His success will come through his own faith in himself.

### Card 7: The Moon

The Moon in the position of romance, beauty, and desire indicated that Kyle has a strong feminine side to his nature, which makes him sensitive and creative in addition to having a practical side. This was corroborated astrologically by the fact that in his chart Venus was found in the sign of Taurus, an extremely practical earth sign that grounded his love of beauty (Venus) while his Moon was in the extra-sensitive sign of Pisces, which is linked with creativity, art, music, and compassion.

### Card 6: Six of Wands

In the position of new insights, this card indicates Kyle will triumph over adversity and be victorious in his endeavors. He will overcome what opposes him, and his self-doubt will be resolved, indicating success and recognition.

### Card 5: The Chariot

In the position of struggle and activity, The Chariot indicated that Kyle was going to have to work hard to harness both sides of his nature, the practical and the dreamy. This card also shows that he'd have to put effort into convincing his wife that his plans would also benefit her so that she would become his partner and not oppose his wishes, which would be destructive to him.

### Card 4: Four of Pentacles

Money has always been an issue for Kyle, as shown by this card appearing in the position of abundance and memories. He came from a modest home where each penny had to be carefully counted, and there were none to spare. He worked his way through school with great difficulty and still has painful memories of frugal living. To solve his issues of abundance, he has to have faith in himself, as was already indicated by Card 8, and perform daily affirmations to strengthen his inner belief in his value as a musician.

### Card 3: The High Priestess

In the position of creativity, receptivity, and limits, The High Priestess indicates that Kyle has much talent that is yet to be developed. At the moment, he is suffering limitations because he has not delved deeply into himself to discover what he can do, but he is receptive to the idea of uncovering and utilizing his creative abilities to the greatest extent possible. As the moon rules The High Priestess, this card is an echo of Card 7, The Moon, and encourages him to express himself fully.

### Card 2: The Wheel of Fortune

This card appearing in the position of goals, changes, and power indicates that Kyle has already put the wheel of change into motion by his intense desire to pursue his musical career. Whether he is fully aware of the process or not, his vivid fantasies of the kind of life he wants to live have already served to get his subconscious mind to work to make it happen. Kyle is going to make this change and reach his goal—because his inner self is directing him and has already taken charge. There is no turning back now.

### Card 1: Ace of Wands

In the outcome position, the Ace of Wands indicates that Kyle is starting in a new work/career direction and that all will turn out well. All kinds of new opportunities will come his way, and new contacts will be helpful. His excitement about making this life-changing move will carry him to success.

## HOROSCOPE SPREAD

In this spread, twelve cards are laid out in a circle and each card corresponds to one of the twelve houses of the astrological chart. A thirteenth card, a Significator, can be placed in the center if desired.

# HOUSES

House One begins at the nine o'clock position, and the cards are dealt counterclockwise. Each house refers to a specific area of life; thus, the cards are read in reference to the house in which they fall. This spread is not generally used to answer specific questions—it provides an overview of the person's life at the time of the reading. The querent's sun sign or birth chart are not factors in a reading that uses this spread.

### The First House: The Self

The first house refers to the physical body and appearance, as well as the querent's vitality, identity, sense of self, and the immediate impression he makes on others.

### The Second House: Personal Resources

The second house shows what the querent considers valuable. This includes money, personal possessions, resources, earning ability, and the person's identification with what he owns.

### The Third House: The Near Environment

The third house covers three areas of life that at first may not seem related, but taken together represent normal daily life, what astrologers call the near environment—communications related to the routine of everyday life; involvement with friends, neighbors, siblings, and the community at large; and short-distance travel in one's near environment.

### The Fourth House: Roots

The fourth house represents the foundation of one's life—home, family, parents (especially the mother), tradition, heritage, the past, one's homeland—in short, the querent's roots.

### The Fifth House: Self-Expression

The fifth house shows the querent's creative and self-expressive side, which may play out as artistic endeavors, romantic relationships, hobbies and amusements, or children.

### The Sixth House: Health and Service

The sixth house relates to health, health-oriented routines including nutrition and exercise, and the link between work and health. It also describes the querent's daily work or chores, duties, job-oriented relationships, service to others, and the capacity for self-sacrifice.

### The Seventh House: One-on-One Relationships

Traditionally the house of marriage and partnerships, the seventh represents all one-on-one relationships—business and personal, including relationships with enemies.

### The Eighth House: Transformation

The eighth is the house of the past, transformative change, death, inheritance, and other people's resources. In this case, death usually refers to the end of something old so that something new can emerge. The eighth house also shows how another's resources affect you.

### The Ninth House: Higher Knowledge

The ninth house represents the higher mind, philosophy, religion/spirituality, the law, and advanced education, as well as long-distance travel, especially to foreign lands. This house shows the querent's search for meaning and how he goes about expanding his horizons.

### The Tenth House: Life Task

The tenth house represents social or professional status, career, public image, and parents (the father especially). Authority, responsibilities, honor, and reputation are tenth-house matters, too.

### The Eleventh House: Friendships

The eleventh house refers to the querent's friends and groups with which he is affiliated. Goals, hopes, and wishes are shown by this house, too.

### The Twelfth House: The Hidden Realm

The twelfth house represents that which is hidden, or not yet revealed, including our dreams and fantasies. It also reveals the querent's latent talents as well as fears, weaknesses, secrets, and unknown enemies. Because matters associated with this sector are often unknown to us, the house is sometimes connected with self-undoing.

## AN EXAMPLE OF A HOROSCOPE SPREAD

The querent, Alison, was a woman in her mid-forties, married with a four-year-old daughter. She worked full-time in an academic job at a university, appeared healthy, and was of a cheerful disposition. Her husband's work required him to travel, and he was away from home much of the time.

### House 1: The Sun, reversed

This card showed that Alison's natural optimism and sunny disposition were being affected by her life situation, which was yet to be revealed by the remaining cards. She was suffering from low self-esteem but trying to maintain a façade of cheerfulness and normality. However, something was clearly wrong.

### House 2: Page of Cups

This card referred to her daughter, who had been asking questions about why daddy was never home. Alison replied that her father was away working (which was true), but the child was nonetheless delivering a message to her mother that she sensed in her heart (Cups) that the family situation was amiss. Her child was the most important person in Alison's life, and her welfare was essential.

### House 3: Eight of Swords

This card indicated that communications were being blocked, and Alison was in a quandary as to what to do about the situation. She and her husband hardly ever talked about anything important; he had withdrawn from communication with her, and she felt helpless.

### House 4: The Tower, reversed

The appearance of the reversed Tower indicated that Alison was trying to hold on to the crumbling structure of her home life. The situation was exacerbated by her husband's constant traveling, which Alison thought was a means to avoid confronting their marital problems for the sake of her daughter.

### House 5: Ten of Wands

This card suggested that Alison was carrying a burden that was preventing her from enjoying life. She had shouldered total care for their daughter and resented her husband's absences and lack of concern for the little girl, which made her feel like a single parent. She felt alone with heavy responsibilities and had little time for socializing or fun.

### House 6: Three of Swords

This card indicated some kind of separation from a work situation that was unsatisfactory. It turned out that Alison was in the process of changing jobs, to a new department within the university, which would be less stressful than her present position.

### House 7: King of Swords, reversed

This card represented Alison's husband, who was an Aquarius, the fixed Air sign. It showed his rigid mental attitudes toward the marriage and his unwillingness to open up and talk to her due to his desire to avoid messy emotional scenes. This card illustrated that the marriage was over and existed in name only. Alison confessed that she and her husband had been using separate bedrooms for several months.

### House 8: The Empress, reversed

This card suggested that a past issue involving pregnancy or a maternal figure was involved in the situation. Alison admitted the only reason she had married was that she had become pregnant. When she discovered herself pregnant, her husband did the right thing but subsequently was not much interested in the child he hadn't wanted or planned for.

### House 9: The Star

This card indicated Alison would have great success in her academic career and/or that she would pursue other forms of consciousness-raising. She said she was happy with the prospect of the new job, which carried much prestige, but also she was interested in pursuing metaphysics, such as astrology and Tarot, and learning one of the healing arts, Reiki.

### House 10: The World

This happy card in Alison's tenth house of career assured that the job change was a smart career move and that she would be happy and successful with it. She verified that the new job was the single really bright spot in her life at the time.

### House 11: King of Wands

This card represented the head of Alison's new department who had asked her to lead a task force in her specialty, which meant she would be involved with group activities. The King indicated her leadership style would be forthright and masculine rather than subtle and feminine. Success was assured.

### House 12: The Moon

The Moon appearing in the twelfth house indicated that Alison needed time by herself to get in touch with her deepest feelings, to access her intuitive self, to step back from the pressures of work and taking care of her daughter to process her feelings about her marriage situation before deciding what action to take. She needed to consult her own inner feminine wisdom rather than relying on an intellectual, rational approach to her marriage problem.

## FENG SHUI SPREAD

This pattern represents the eight-sided octagon called a bagua, used by Feng Shui practitioners to examine the connections between a person's home and his/her life. The cards show the energies and influences operating in each area of the querent's life.

*Card 1:* Fame, future, career

*Card 2:* Relationships, marriage, partnerships

*Card 3:* Creativity, children

*Card 4:* Helpful people, friends, agents/associates/colleagues, travel

*Card 5:* Self, identity, image

*Card 6:* Wisdom, knowledge, spirituality

*Card 7:* Family, community, neighbors

*Card 8:* Wealth

*Card 9:* Health

## EXAMPLE OF A FENG SHUI SPREAD

The querent was Eric, a software designer in his mid-thirties who had just relocated to California after living in the Midwest for most of his life. He wanted to know what he could expect as a result of this move.

### Card 1: Eight of Pentacles

In the fame/future/career position, this card indicates that Eric could succeed if he was willing to work hard and sincerely pursue his goals.

### Card 2: Three of Swords

This card reveals part of the reason for Eric's move—a divorce. He had decided to start over by putting distance between himself and his former wife, but the separation was causing him pain, and he felt lonely and alienated from the people he cared about.

### Card 3: Ace of Wands

The Ace of Wands indicates that Eric is starting a new job that excites him and stimulates his creativity. He'll have many interesting and challenging opportunities available to him in this new position.

### Card 4: The Hermit

The card of isolation and introspection, The Hermit in this spot showed that Eric might have a hard time making new friends and could find himself alone much of the time. However, he needed to get in touch with himself, do some soul-searching, and discover his real path in life, rather than surrounding himself with family and friends.

### Card 5: King of Swords

Although Eric knew he was intelligent and creative, he hadn't yet had a chance to show what he could do in his field. This card suggested that the move to California and his new job would enable Eric to express his knowledge and skills and gain self-confidence as a result.

### Card 6: Page of Pentacles

This card in the position of wisdom/knowledge indicates that Eric could benefit from taking classes or improving his practical skills.

### Card 7: Seven of Swords

A card of movement and intellectual freedom, the Seven of Swords shows that Eric had left his old home and family to strike out on his own in an area that would allow him more independence. As a result of his relocation, Eric hoped to find like-minded people and opportunities that weren't available to him in his former location. However, this card also reminded him not to make waves in his new community.

### Card 8: The Magician

In the wealth position, this trump suggests that Eric needs to use his intelligence, skills, and willpower to accomplish his financial goals. Much depends on his attitude and how he utilizes his knowledge to earn money.

### Card 9: Four of Swords

This card, in the position of health, shows that Eric has been under a lot of stress due to his recent divorce and relocation. He needs to rest and recuperate, or he could run the risk of illness.

## THIRTEEN-CARD STORY SPREAD

This method describes the evolution of a situation over a period of time. After shuffling and cutting the deck, lay out thirteen cards in three rows, as shown in the illustration.

**Card 1:** *The birth of the subject of the reading.*

**Cards 2 through 11:** *The development of the situation—positive and negative conditions, opportunities and obstacles, progress and setbacks. The linear pattern lets you see how each step has led to the next and how they influence the current concern.*

**Card 12:** *The near future.*

**Card 13:** *The more distant future.*

# AN EXAMPLE OF A THIRTEEN-CARD STORY SPREAD

Harry, a man in his early sixties, was considering retiring, but he had concerns about turning over the family business to his son.

## Card 1: Two of Pentacles

This card represents Harry's business, a printing company, which he and his brother had started more than three decades ago and built into a successful company.

## Card 2: Five of Swords

During the early years of operation, the two brothers had often disagreed about how to grow the business. Harry, being more conservative than his brother, wanted to move slowly and at times he felt they'd taken too many risks and overextended themselves.

## Card 3: Five of Pentacles

At times, money had been tight and had caused cautious, security-conscious Harry much distress.

## Card 4: Eight of Pentacles

Through hard work, determination, and conscientious business practices, Harry and his brother had managed to make their printing company a stable, reputable operation.

## Card 5: Knight of Wands, reversed

Harry's brother, a salesman and optimist, had convinced Harry to branch out into other areas and to open new locations. However, their plans failed when the economy took a dive. It took years for them to recoup their losses, which left Harry feeling very wary about making changes. The lingering memories of loss and failure were at the root of his present fears about giving the reins to his son.

## Card 6: Ten of Swords

This card reveals a period of difficulty and stress, as Harry and his brother struggled to hold onto their company and pay off debts.

### Card 7: Death

This card shows the death of Harry's brother, due to a heart attack. Harry believed that overwork and stress had contributed to his brother's early demise. Because Harry was beginning to experience health problems himself, he wanted to retire, before he was too old to enjoy himself.

### Card 8: King of Pentacles

This card represents Harry, now the sole head of the family business.

### Card 9: Page of Swords

After the death of his brother, Harry brought his son into the company. Swords suggest the nature of the business—communication— but this card also reveal the son's sense of insecurity and inexperience.

### Card 10: The Chariot

Harry still feels a need to control the business. His son has some good ideas for updating the company by adding new equipment and techniques, but Harry is reluctant to take risks. This card shows the two men need to work together cooperatively for the good of the company.

### Card 11: The Hanged Man

This card signifies the present and advises Harry to let go and allow his son to take over the business. Harry needs to learn to trust that all will be well.

### Card 12: Nine of Pentacles

As the card of the near future, the Nine of Pentacles clearly indicates that the business is sound and will continue to prosper.

### Card 13: Ten of Pentacles

The more distant future looks bright, too. The Ten of Pentacles represents family money and security, so this reading assured Harry that he could feel confident in his son's ability to run the company successfully.

# THE TAROT FOR PERSONAL DEVELOPMENT

Many people believe that the Tarot is a valuable resource for personal growth and can reveal important psychological issues you need to address. Encoded within the symbols and imagery of the Tarot are keys that can unlock the doors of perception, so that you may see your own life and the path to higher knowledge more clearly. Many Tarot scholars believe the Major Arcana was designed as a course in initiation, presented in twenty-two stages: the trump cards. But the Minor Arcana, too, is a rich body of information that you can draw upon for personal development. This chapter will discuss using the Tarot as a method to further your personal growth and develop a deeper connection with your intuition.

# DAILY INSIGHTS FROM THE TAROT

Many people turn to the Tarot for daily insights. Each morning, you can shuffle your favorite deck, ask for guidance, and draw a single card. Sometimes this card will shed light on a problem, project, or issue you're dealing with in your life. Sometimes it may present the theme for the day. Or it may point to a matter you need to pay attention to. On and off throughout the day, you can think about the card you drew that morning and how it relates to what unfolds during the day. You can even place the card in a spot where you will see it often and reflect upon its meaning, letting its message guide you.

It may appear that you're selecting cards entirely at random, but there's nothing arbitrary or chance about it. Your subconscious and/or your Higher Self are presenting information in this elegant way, and the cards you pick each day are never irrelevant.

During particularly significant periods, you might draw the same card again and again over a span of a week, a month, or more. Like a dream that keeps repeating, this suggests that the same forces are operating in your life and that you need to keep working on the issues indicated by the card.

As you work on specific areas of your life, you'll see your growth reflected in the cards you draw. For instance, you might pick the Ace of Pentacles when you start a moneymaking venture. As the project bears fruit, you might draw the Seven of Pentacles, which shows you are beginning to see the results of your efforts.

It's a good idea to keep a journal or log of your daily readings. Note the date, what's going on in your life, and any particular concerns or areas of interest. Write down insights or questions that come to you in connection with the card or cards you draw each day. Periodically, you may wish to look back at the cards you drew previously to see how a matter has evolved or how your knowledge has grown over time. Something that was unclear to you before might make sense now. In this way, you can follow your progress and understand how the Tarot is guiding you along your path.

# DAILY AFFIRMATIONS AND THE TAROT

You can also use the Tarot to inspire personal growth in much the same way as you would use affirmations. An affirmation is a short, positive statement that describes a condition or change you wish to produce. An example of an affirmation is: "My life is rich with abundance of all kinds." An affirmation may be a phrase you coin yourself, a quote by someone you respect, or a sentence from a book. By repeating the affirmation regularly, you reprogram your subconscious and, in time, bring about the desired result.

Tarot cards can function as visual affirmations. Let's say, for example, you want to find a romantic partner. Select the Two of Cups or The Lovers from your deck and gaze at it while you contemplate your intention. If you like, you can display the card where you will see it often. Each time you look at it, you'll be reminded of your objective.

You can work on developing inner qualities in the same way. Choose The High Priestess if you want to improve your intuition. Strength can help you increase your personal power and confidence. The Queen of Cups is good for encouraging flexibility and acceptance.

Although you can work on more than one goal at a time, it's usually best to limit yourself to a few that you consider most urgent or important. Choose cards that represent the end result(s) you desire. Spend at least a few minutes each day contemplating the card(s) you've chosen, allowing the symbols to imprint themselves on your subconscious. If you wish, you can combine the cards with verbal affirmations—stare at the card while you repeat your affirmation aloud. You're more likely to get fast, effective results if you combine the two techniques.

Some Tarot decks are designed specifically for this purpose. The Tarot Affirmations deck, for instance, combines the imagery of the Universal Waite pack with selected affirmations and sayings. Each card is printed with several inspirational thoughts that relate to the meaning of the card.

# REFLECTING ON THE MAJOR ARCANA FOR INNER TRUTHS

It would be hard to find a more appropriate tool for spiritual and personal growth than the Major Arcana. For centuries, seekers have used this body of occult wisdom to access hidden knowledge and to connect with the higher realms. These powerful images portray archetypes that exist within the collective unconscious and that connect us to something larger than ourselves. At the spiritual level, each of the Major Arcana cards represents a state of being, or an inner truth about yourself.

The simplest way to understand the Major Arcana in spiritual terms is to think of it as an ascending staircase with twenty-two steps. Each card represents a lesson you must learn, a boundary you must cross in order to move up to the next step. And you have to figure out how to do this yourself; there is no set system. Each step leads to the next and is a little different than the one before it. Each has a different lesson to impart. Some are wider or narrower than others; some are smoother or rougher. The time you spend on each step is up to you. You'll know when you're ready to move up to the next step because you will have understood the meaning of the previous one.

You can either study the trump cards in consecutive order, or choose individual cards that represent areas or concepts you wish to work on, in whatever order suits your purposes. Or separate the Major Arcana from the entire deck, shuffle, and draw a card for study, letting your inner knowing guide you.

<><><><><><><><><><><><><><><><><><><><><><><><><><><><><><><><><><><><><><><><><><>

You can recite this if you want to practice meditating on the Tarot with prayer: "Everything that I believe to be true about the Spirit, I understand is also true about myself. Its Goodness is my goodness. Its Power is my power. Its Presence in me is my true self. There is only one True Self."

<><><><><><><><><><><><><><><><><><><><><><><><><><><><><><><><><><><><><><><><><><>

If, for example, you wish to discover the source of inner strength, pick the Strength card. Start by simply gazing at the card, without analyzing it. Let the colors, pictures, and symbols connect with your intuition and reveal themselves to you gradually, before you begin to examine the images more carefully.

In her companion book to *The Sacred Circle Tarot*, Anna Franklin suggests you approach the card as if you were going to enter it, like walking through a doorway, and interact with the scenario depicted there. Don't just see the images, try to experience them. Allow your senses to come into play. Feel the sun on your face, the grass under your feet. Witness the murkiness and mystery connected with The Moon or the burning sensation of anger, jealousy, obsession, and fear depicted by The Devil.

Write down what you glean from your study—your insights, awarenesses, questions, impressions, and feelings. Notice how the energies represented by the cards are playing out in your own life—or how you would like to be able express them. Because the trump cards are quite complex, it's probably best to limit your study to one card at a time, until you understand it—even if it takes several days or weeks.

# WORKING WITH THE MINOR ARCANA

The cards in the Minor Arcana represent everyday concerns and earthly matters. For example, the suit of Cups represents the emotions and relationships, Pentacles stand for financial and physical conditions, Swords symbolize mental issues and communication, and Wands are linked with creativity, spiritual considerations, and willpower.

Determine which suit covers the issue or situation you wish to work on first. Then, pick the card within that suit that speaks most directly to your objective. (See Part 2 for interpretations of the Minor Arcana cards.) For instance, if your goal is to rekindle the love and affection in a romantic relationship, select the Six of Cups from your deck.

Begin by gazing at the card for a minute or two, without attempting to analyze it. Just let the colors, symbols, and so on impress themselves on your subconscious. Note any thoughts, feelings, or insights that arise into your awareness and write them down in your Tarot journal.

Each person's responses will be different—and your own responses will vary from day to day—so simply jot down whatever comes to you without censoring yourself, even if it doesn't make sense immediately.

---

The Six of Cups in the Waite deck has a large cup that rests on a pillar decorated with an X, which is the rune for love. Runes are ancient glyphs or symbols that are often carved on stones, wood, or bone, and used as a tool for consulting the deities.

---

Next, examine the card more closely. Contemplate the symbols depicted on the card to ascertain their meanings. In most storytelling decks, for example, the Six of Cups shows a young man and woman (sometimes a male and a female child) in a pleasant setting—a peaceful village, or a sunny meadow in the country. Their youth is one of the keys to understanding the card—innocence and openness are necessary for love to flourish. The colors are cheerful and bright, signifying optimism. The image is one of generosity, comfort, companionship, and joy. Often the six cups pictured on the card are filled with flowers, a familiar symbol of love. Sometimes the male is portrayed offering one of the cups to the female as a token of affection, which indicates that sharing, giving of oneself, and being receptive—give and take—are essential in any partnership.

What symbols do you see on your own card? Some decks are more symbol-rich than others. What individual and universal meanings do they hold? It may help to make a list of the symbols you notice and your interpretations of them. Continue studying the card you've selected until you've uncovered all the information you feel is relevant at this time. After a day or two, revisit the same card to see if you can glean additional insights from it. If you own more than one deck, examine the same card in each deck. One card may reveal something that was not apparent in another.

## ONE SUIT AT A TIME

Working your way through one suit at a time is a good way to develop a deeper understanding of the four fundamental energies present in our world and the areas of life associated with them. Begin with the suit that represents the area in which you'd most like to expand your knowledge and select the Ace from that suit. Aces depict pure, primal, focused, core energies; each Ace contains the raw nature of the suit to which it belongs. Study the symbolism on the card. In the Waite deck, a disembodied hand extends from the clouds and offers you the Ace, as if a divine being were handing you a gift. What do the other symbols and images on the card mean to you?

Next, examine the Two in the suit you've chosen. The Two suggests polarity, duality, self versus other, and a need for balance, cooperation, and harmony. In some decks, the illustration on the Two of Pentacles shows a juggler trying to handle two balls. What do you notice in the card you've chosen? What feelings or impressions arise as you gaze at the card?

Continue in this manner until you've worked through the entire suit, progressing at your own pace. Some people are comfortable studying one card a day; others may move more slowly. Perhaps you'll prefer to familiarize yourself with several cards at a time, noting the way each builds on the energy of its predecessor. Allow your analytical mind and your intuition to inform you. Keep a record of your thoughts and insights as you study the cards, along with information about how the elemental qualities represented are being expressed in your own life.

# CONNECT WITH YOUR INTUITION

In any kind of divinatory work, intuition is an important factor. Some methods such as tea-leaf reading or crystal-ball gazing could be considered low data/high subjectivity, meaning there is little hard data to go on, and your intuition plays a major role in interpreting the results. In high data/low subjectivity systems, like astrology and the Tarot, the use of a physical tool (i.e., the birth chart or the cards) provides a more clearly defined form of reliable information on which to base your interpretations.

However, even in the case of these data-rich systems, personal intuition is a vital component of an accurate reading. The symbolic nature of these systems allows for the possibility of interpretation on many different levels. Therefore, it is important to spend time and effort learning to communicate with your intuition. Meditation is a time-honored practice for developing a strong connection with your inner self. Dream work, too, can enhance your intuitive abilities.

It is precisely the holistic nature of intuition that gives it its power. In your unconscious, you have a huge data bank of experiences upon which to draw, even though you aren't aware of most of them. You know much more than you think you know, and your intuition can enable you to access this dormant knowledge.

Developing intuitive skills should be fun, not a chore. If your practice becomes monotonous, change the time or place for your meditations. Your sixth sense is part of who you are. Therefore, your moods, intelligence, education, interests, health, state of mind, past experiences, future aims, and ability to be open to the experiences and the time of day and setting—the "furniture of the mind" as author Willa Cather called it—can all affect how your intuition performs. Some people will naturally be more intuitive than others—psychic ability is like any other skill. And, like any other skill, it will improve with use.

How long it will take is up to you. Much depends on your personal goals, the quality and length of time you invest, individual aptitude, and factors as yet unknown. Sometimes people work diligently for a long time and nothing seems to be happening and then, bingo!—a portal appears. It's like walking along a dull, dreary street and suddenly passing through a gate into a beautiful, flower-filled courtyard hidden behind the façade of a building. As you learn to trust your psychic responses and let them operate on their own, success becomes automatic. You'll wonder how you ever got along without this valuable skill!

## USE THE TAROT TO IMPROVE YOUR INTUITION

There are many ways to discover your own inner dimensions. One of the best of these is the contemplation of symbols, and the Tarot is full of symbols. Symbols speak directly to the unconscious. Meditating on the cards' symbols awakens the corresponding archetypal forms embedded in the unconscious, and that in turn allows you to arrive at the right interpretation, to see the truth in the heart of the matter. By reflecting on the deep meanings of the symbols on a regular basis, you set in motion an inward process that will reveal to you truths about yourself and enable you to look outward to grasp Universal Truth.

If you want to build your predictive skills, try using the cards to predict the outcome of something that you will know tomorrow, such as the winner of a ball game or a political election. Keep track of your hits. Over time, your success rate will likely improve.

If you have a particular issue or concern about which you want advice, concentrate on that issue. Write it down in the form of a question, if you wish. Sit quietly, close your eyes, and hold the question or concern in your mind. Draw a card from your deck and look at it. Sit still and allow feelings, impressions, or ideas to bubble up into your consciousness. Focus on your breathing if your mind tends to wander. In the beginning, don't ask too much of yourself. Be patient and keep working. Intuition is a natural talent everyone possesses. You cannot fail.

## OTHER WAYS TO DEVELOP INTUITION

Accessing psychic data is a bit like tuning into a radio station. Sometimes you receive information clearly, at other times there's static. Trust and awareness are essential to developing your intuition. If you are not accustomed to doing internal processing in an aware manner, it may take a bit of time for you to get used to doing so. The important thing is to make a commitment to yourself and follow through on it. Don't expect immediate success, but don't rule it out either.

Notice coincidences and pay attention to signs. If you observe or experience something out of the ordinary, or with unusual frequency, take note of it. See if it ties into anything else. If any thoughts pop into your head in conjunction with the sign or coincidence, heed them, too.

During meditation, you empty your mind and allow it to be filled by something other than everyday, rational thinking. You relax into a light trance state and invite input from your Higher Self, subconscious, angels, guides, god, goddess, or whatever term you choose to use. Stilling the mind is easier said than done, however. Some people focus on their breathing, some listen to music, some chant or repeat mantras to quiet their minds. You can also gaze at a meaningful symbol, such as a tattwa or a Tarot card. The objective is to keep your mind and heart open, and to allow insight to flow into your awareness rather than permitting your thoughts to jump about like monkeys in a cage.

Prayer can also connect you with your intuition. Meditation is receptive; prayer is active. It's been said that meditation is listening to god, and prayer is speaking to Him. Praying puts us into an altered state of consciousness not unlike the ones used for self-hypnosis and visualization. When we pray, we are actually visualizing the result desired, even if we are not doing this consciously. It is a good idea to begin each Tarot session with a short prayer affirming your innate connection to Spirit and your faith in divine guidance.

# GLOSSARY OF TERMS

**Arcana**
Secret knowledge.

**Court cards**
The four "people" cards in each suit of the Minor Arcana, the Court cards consist of a king, queen, knight (or prince), and page (or princess).

**Divination**
The act of predicting the future, often with the aid of a device such as the Tarot, runes, etc.

**Element**
One of the four fundamental energies in the universe—Earth, Air, Fire, and Water. Each element corresponds to one suit of the Tarot.

**Feng Shui**
The ancient Chinese art of placement, pronounced "fung shway."

**Kabbalah**
An ancient Hebrew mystical tradition to which the Tarot has many links. Also spelled Cabala, Qabala, and other variations.

**Karma**
A concept of cause and effect, as taught in some Eastern religions.

**Major Arcana**
One of the two books of the Tarot, consisting of twenty-two cards beginning with The Fool and ending with The World.

## Minor Arcana
One of the two books of the Tarot, usually consisting of forty numbered cards and sixteen Court cards divided into four suits—Wands, Pentacles, Cups, and Swords.

## Occult
Hidden or secret.

## Pip cards
The numbered cards in the Tarot deck.

## Querent
Someone who asks a question or seeks information. In a Tarot reading, the querent is the person consulting the cards.

## Reading
A consultation using Tarot cards to gain insight or information.

## Significator
A card chosen to represent the person for whom the reading is being done.

## Spread
A pattern used in a Tarot reading to reveal insight or to answer a question.

# INDEX